A Bunch of Ellipses...

Two Plays
by
Andrew Heller

Dedication

For Max, you did it buddy, you helped me heal ...

Acknowledgements

Patty Burton
Dr. T. Paul Pfeiffer
Music, Theatre, and Dance Department of Salisbuy University
Adam Adkins
Courtney Blackford
Jessica Reneé Brunk
Zachary Coffman
Karen Lewis
Danielle R. Slater
Steven Young
Alice Teresa Bliss and the North Street Playhouse
Jennifer Ferguson
Patty Gregorio

And a few very special thank yous to
Stephanie Fowler, Mike Parker, and Sam Heller...
your love and support and foot in the behind are all I ever need!

Author's Note

I remember pacing the hall and hanging out by the bathroom door in our condo/patio home we rented in Nashville, TN while my wife lay in the tub and read the very first draft of the very first version of what began as a play called Coconut Cake. I held my breath and my heart would not beat, yet would race to life as I took in that precious air every time I heard her laugh. It was a start of putting pen to paper or words to form as a means of working through my own sense of loss and fear and inadequacy as a husband, father, brother, and son.

I approached Coconut Cake again, with a different title, and then a different title after that. Several of my students at the local university where I taught workshopped these two plays for me. We read, and discussed, and I would re-wright and do it all again the next day. Eventually we did a public reading of the two plays. And I felt as though I still had work to do, more to write, more to say.

At times I hoped these words would help explain all I wished to say — or shout or scream — from the deepest depths within my soul. They were filled with all the angst and anxieties ... and intentions of fixing the very things inside that brought them to life. Several drafts and versions and titles later, and after several other adaptations of other works, plays, poetry, and even a young adult mystery series ... I have revisited these works.

I approached them once again at a time of desperation. And once again I looked to them as a fix. But as I recrafted and rewrote and revisited the words, the thoughts, the characters that had become so real to me; as I allowed myself to approach those fears and inadequacies, I realized that one does not write to fix. Or perhaps they do ... but writing ain't fixing. Writing is healing. And healing is not a fix. Healing leaves scabs that we constantly pick and open and let bleed again. Healing leaves scars that forever change the topography of not just the flesh, but our soul as well. And healing changes; it changes thought, and perspective, and memory, and heart.

And so here we are, after nearly a score of years, I've picked these scabs and I've let my heart bleed all over again. I've reintroduced myself to these characters and they have spoken to me once more. Their words are different to me now, and the characters have somehow become a little changed from what I remember ... but I've changed, times have changed, and perspective certainly has evolved. I've healed and broken and healed a thousand times from a thousand different wounds ... but these words of mine, they still haven't fixed a darn thing, ha!

- Andrew Heller

86 Proof

For LNA ...

86 Proof

Characters:

Daddy: 64 very sick, recovering from an accident

Rachael: 36, divorced, takes care of Daddy

Jeremy: 34, brother of Rachael and Loretta, married to Elaine, lives out of town, they have four children

Loretta: 27, baby sister to Rachael and Jeremy, Lesbian

Elaine: 32, married to Jeremy, four kids, one on the way

Setting:

The play takes place in the home of Rachael and Daddy. Daddy is ill and has lived with Rachael since the death of Mom three years ago. All of the action takes place in the Living Room of Rachael's home. There is a Dining area with a pass through Kitchen. There is an entrance to the Kitchen, the Front Door, a Stairway to the second floor, and a Hallway leading to a den and a bathroom. There is nothing notable about the furnishings, it is tasteful, not new not old. Everything is rather neat and tidy, everything has a place. Pictures of family are very prominent. They hang on the wall, are on end tables, everywhere.

Act I scene i: The Arrival

The scene opens with Daddy coming from the hallway and crossing up the stairs. He slowly climbs the stairs with some effort, and disappears down the hall. Rachael enters from the front door with groceries and crosses to the kitchen. She can be seen through the pass through putting the groceries away. Daddy reappears from the upstairs hallway carrying some books, a picture, and a lamp from his room upstairs. As he nears the bottom of the stairs he drops the lamp and falls. Rachael comes running.

Rachael: Oh my God! What are you doing!?! What happened?!

Daddy: Nothing! Go away.

Rachael: What do you mean nothing? You're lying at the bottom of the stairs with a pile of books on top of you! Why are you doing this, you know better than that, let me help you! *Tries to help him up, but he won't let her*

Daddy: Stop, stop, shut up talking. Let go of me. Help me up!

Rachael: You could have killed yourself, you know!

Daddy: Don't get too excited, my day's commin'. *picking up picture, muttering to himself* Damn picture broke.

Rachael: Are you hurt?

Daddy: It's a picture of me and your mother. *handing picture to Rachel*

Rachael: And I asked if you were hurt. Daddy, are you hurt?

Daddy: This was taken a long time ago, you know.

Rachael: Daddy! Why ... *starts to ask about the picture* Are you hurt?!?

Daddy: Damn she was sweet, you know. A fine looking woman. And was she ever fun! *now standing with Rachael's help* Of course that was before we had all you little brats.

Rachael: You're fine.

Daddy: Get off of me. Jeez.

Rachael: Daddy ...

Daddy: And don't start nagging ...

Rachael: Daddy ...

Daddy: Nag, nag, nag, nag, nag. *walking away, taking the picture with him*

Rachael: Daddy! Stand still and look at me!

Daddy: And disagreeable too! Do me a favor, would you, and pick that mess up and take it into the den.

Rachael: For the life of me, I don't understand you. Why are you doing this? Why are you moving this stuff? You're not going to answer me. Why would I think you would answer me? You would just as soon talk to some damn picture ... *he shoots her a look, she changes the subject and goes to him* Would you please come over here and sit down? You scared me half to death, you know. Are you sure you are alright?

Daddy: I'm fine, let go of me, I don't want to sit down.

Rachael: I'm not nagging, but I did tell you that you didn't need to move down here until you were ready. You know I only want you down here because the stairs are too difficult for you, but if you aren't ready to move, then we can wait. And when you are ready, I will help you carry your things down stairs, or we could ask Jeremy to help, or Lo. She says she is coming this weekend by the way, I don't know, maybe she will. You know Lo.

Daddy: Would you shut up and stop following me?

Rachael: What is wrong with you? You have been acting like this all day. I really don't understand you.

Daddy: And I told you that I didn't want everyone coming here this weekend, not now ...

Rachael: Daddy, we've been through this. I don't want to go through this again. Besides, it's not like I can do anything now, they'll be here any minute. Give me the picture, I'll put it away with your things.

Daddy: Just put the other stuff away. I need this right now.

Rachel: Well I don't. Let's put it away. *she tries to take it, he won't let her*

Daddy: So, are you going to pick on everyone this weekend? Huh? You know, in your own sweet way you are so God damned mean. You always were. Even as a child. You were a scary child.

Rachael: Oh, and where does that come from? Did I say anything? I can't, for the life of me ...

Daddy: Mean.

Rachael: Not now Daddy, please, you are sick, you are under a lot of stress, we both are. You need help, and I need a little help too. So please ... if we work together ...

Daddy: Stop talking to me like I am some child, stop treating me like I am some damn invalid.

Rachael: Daddy, I know that you are not a child. With a child I might have more patience. What you are is a spoiled rotten sick old man who acts like a child. If you want, I can drop the niceties, I can be mean if you really want me to ... but every time I do it only makes us both upset. *he gives her the picture* So here we are. *Rachel sets the picture face down on a table while picking up some of the dropped things* Jeremy is going to be here anytime now ... oh! And he's bringing Elaine. I forgot to tell you. I told him not to, and I didn't think he was going to, but apparently she changed his mind and ...

Daddy: God Damnit!!!

Rachael: Daddy ...

Daddy: Is she bringing that entire litter? I don't have time for them damn kids. I don't feel well!

Rachael: No, they are not bringing your precious grandchildren. I am sorry to disappoint you, but we thought it best with things as they are, that the kids not come. I tried to persuade Jeremy to have Elaine stay home too, believe me I did, but apparently she doesn't want to be away from Jeremy right now, and well, I guess I don't blame her.

Daddy: Why? What's wrong with Jeremy?

Rachael: Nothing is wrong with Jeremy.

Daddy: So why does Elaine have to be with him?

Rachael: Well, aside from being his wife, Elaine is due in about 6 weeks.

Daddy: I can't keep up! I didn't know she was in trouble.

Rachael: She's not in trouble, Daddy, she's pregnant.

Daddy: I call that trouble. What is it, five now? Accidents? Surprises? No matter how stupid he is you think he'd figure it out by now. Damn, I had the talk with him! They oughta sew her up or tie him in a knot or both. Jesus, do the math. One plus one equals two, or five, I guess. Five?!?

Rachael: And what makes you think they are all surprises?

Daddy: I've got two that I never wanted.

Rachel: Daddy, there's three of us.

Daddy: Another simple equation.

Rachael: Daddy, do me a favor, just watch a little TV. I'll finish cleaning all of this up. And I will put it in the den, but I am not putting it away. You can do that later. But right now, please just sit there, watch some TV ... there has got to be a game or something on. Just don't do anything until they get here. *Rachael starts picking things up and takes them up stairs, she calls back* ... And don't do anything while they are here!

Daddy: Where are the kids anyway?

Rachael: *from landing* They are with her parents I assume.

Daddy: God damnit! Now why would they go and do a thing like that? Those people are stupider than she is! My grandbabies don't need to be around so many God damn stupid people!

Rachael: Elaine's parents are very nice people, a little reserved perhaps, but very nice. And weren't you the one who said something about her "litter" being here and that perhaps she should be "sewed up"?

Daddy: I'm not talking to you! Nobody likes you anyway, I don't know why you continue to talk! *to himself* Nice people my ass, a bunch of freaks, that's what they are, freaks.

Rachael disappears upstairs, Daddy starts flipping through the channels. Loretta enters through the front door. She is a bit "butch" in appearance, but very pretty. She dresses far younger than her 27 years.

Loretta: You gotta cold beer for an old pal?

Daddy: In the fridge, I need one too, put it in a cup though, the Nazi upstairs doesn't like me to partake. If she catches me, I might end up in the gas chamber.

Loretta: *She crosses into the kitchen and can be seen getting beers.* Wow, Rach had a gas chamber put in? What's the occasion? Small-children move into the neighborhood?

Daddy: There's no occasion, it's only you and Jeremy. I told her she could just use the oven like she always did, but you know Rachael. Never satisfied, always improving upon her technique.

Loretta: She been practicing?

Daddy: She's got me here doesn't she?

Loretta: Ooh, yeah, sorry. So you're looking pretty OK Dad. Sort of. No, not really, you look like shit! What the hell is Rachael doing to you?

Daddy: She's taking care of me. Actually, strike me dead for saying this, but she's trying. It's those damn doctors that are doing it to me. Always giving you pills. They don't even look at you anymore, they just give you these damn pills. And if something doesn't work, they give you more damn pills. I take so many God damn pills my piss is green and my shit is yellow. And speaking of shit, look at yourself. You look like a twelve year old boy. Your hair, your pants. What the hell?

Loretta: *Passing beer through kitchen pass through* Here's your beer, Pop.

Daddy: *Crossing to get beer* You gotta job yet or is Rachael still paying your rent with my money?

Loretta: I put a shot in it.

Daddy: Ah! You were always my favorite. Cheers!

Rachael: *Comes into view from the Landing* Is that you Jeremy? Hi Elaine! Look, I want to give you guys a quick heads up! Loretta may be coming. Well, she says she is anyway, you know how dependable Lo can be. So on top of everything else, we're gonna have all of her stuff to deal with. Anyway, I thought I'd warn you. Lord only knows what she's going to look like this time.

Loretta: *Crosses out of Kitchen and finally sits on couch* Oh shit! Is that bitch coming? I'm outta here. The prodigal son did not return to compete with some nasty, all be it fine, lesbo! *Silence for a moment* How are you Rach? You doing ok? How's the single sexless life treating you? You know, I've got this friend ...

Rachael: *Coming down stairs.* Loretta, Lo, I am so sorry. I ... I am ... so, let's not start this weekend off poorly shall we? Please? Really, I am truly sorry for what I may have said, but as you know I am under a lot of stress right now and I'm sure you are too, I mean you always are, but you know how you get and I just don't want a lot of ... well ... you know what I mean ... so let's at least try to be incident free, OK? Can we do that, please?

Daddy: Nice save! It is uncanny really, your ability to trash someone, get everything off of your chest, apologize and then don't let the other person speak, and then finally, somehow, you manage to insinuate that it's all their God damn fault. You're amazing, you're truly amazing.

Rachel: I don't need it from you either, Daddy.

Daddy: You're just like your Mother.

Rachael: Shut up Daddy. So ... Lo ... how are you?

Loretta: Fine, thanks. You?

Rachael: I am well, thank you for asking. And you, uh, well you look ... as though you are taking care of yourself.

Loretta: Thanks. You don't.

Rachael: How long are you staying?

Loretta: Not long, I hope.

Rachael: Well, this is going well so far. I can see already what a fine weekend we will be having.

Loretta: Yeah, so Elaine is coming? You must be pissed.

Rachael: Why would I be pissed that Elaine is coming? She is my sister-in-law, I am more than happy ...

Loretta: Yeah, right, you can't stand the goody two shoes and you know it.

Rachael: Listen to me Loretta, Elaine and I may not always agree on everything, and that is fine. We are two grown, professional women. Well, I am, she chooses to stay home and have children, and that is her choice. But we ...

Loretta: Hah! See, right there, you don't like her. You don't think she is doing anything worth while.

Rachael: Hmmm, no, it's you that I don't like right now. And what is it you do outside of projecting your own insecurities on other people?

Loretta: Projecting ... now there is a big psychology word.

Rachael: Yes, would you like me to explain what it means?

Loretta: No, I got it covered. I am taking a psychology class at school.

Rachael: Oh, that's right, you decided to go back to school. Didn't Daddy have to pay some old fine to clear your records from your last attempt at a higher education?

Loretta: I might major in it.

Rachael: That's great, Lo, really it is. You can, um, put your things in my room, I guess. Just lie everything on the bed, I'll help you put it away later. You do have things?

Loretta: Yeah, I have things.

Rachael: Good, well that's all set ...

Loretta: But I don't want to stay in your room.

Rachael: Loretta ...

Loretta: Come on Rach, I don't want to put you out. I could bunk with Dad or something ... the couch even?

Rachael: I thought I had already explained things to you, earlier, you know, when we spoke on the phone. Things are in somewhat of a transition right now. There is a transition happening here, and I simply don't have the flexibility to give you your own room. Jeremy and Elaine will have the guest room, I have my room and you will need to share it with me because, well, Daddy is still in his room upstairs, as we are still in the process of moving a few of his things into the den where he is relocating ... but since he is not there yet things are in a bit of disarray, and so that means ...

Daddy: So that means the old man can't get his shit downstairs fast enough. I can take a hint.

Rachael: Now Daddy, you know I didn't mean that as any kind of a hint ...

Daddy: Yeah you did, Lo just isn't bright enough to catch on!

Loretta: Oh please, I just like to watch her squirm.

Daddy: Come on Lo, can you help an old man move all his worldly possessions to his new cell? You just like to watch her squirm ... that is exactly why you have always been my favorite. Damn you're funny.

Loretta and Daddy exit upstairs laughing.
Rachael busies herself with putting the rest of the things away. She picks up the picture from the table sits on the couch and begins to cry.
Loretta enters with a box of Daddy's things.

Loretta: So Frau Strict-n-mean, does the furniture have to go too? Or are you gonna make the old man sleep on the ... hey, what's wrong?

Rachael: No, no, nothing, no furniture, just his things ... I had some new furniture put into the den for him. It came last week actually. He has all new things, even one of those adjustable beds so he can sit up and watch television. His new television. He has everything he needs to be ... *under her breath and putting the picture behind a pillow* oh Lord, I can't do this ... I am fine, I am fine. Jeremy and Elaine will be here soon, and I'm still trying to get dinner together ...

Loretta: Rach ... what is it? Talk to me big sister ... what can I do?

Rachael: Just help Daddy with his things ... or set the table ... or ... *door bell rings* That must be Jeremy and Elaine. Why don't you help them?

Rachael goes into the kitchen and busies herself with dinner.
Loretta, a bit confused watches her sister leave.
Enter Elaine.

Elaine: Oh my word, I really need to find the little girl's room, I am sorry to be so rude, but please, I forgot which way, where ...

Loretta: Oh, hi, um, down the hall to the left ... Holy shit Elaine!

Elaine: *Exiting down hall.* Oh I know, the doctor says this one could come early! Isn't it exciting?

Loretta: Sure ... if getting fat and squeezing a pumpkin out of your body is your idea of exciting.

Jeremy: Hey, Lo, wow, good to see you! Rach said you might be here. I wasn't sure if you'd come.

Loretta: Jesus Christ! Why does everyone think I'm so friggin' unreliable?

Jeremy: Easy girl! So how are ya?

Loretta: Good enough to get the Rachael treatment in less than five minutes. Let's see how long you last.

Jeremy: Oh man, sorry. Beat you to it, I got it without even being here.

Loretta: No way. Her evil mind powers reach all the way across the state?

Jeremy: Quite possibly they do, but I got it over the phone. I get it every time she calls. The kids are a great excuse to get off the phone though, "Hey Rach, gotta go, the kids are about to blow something up."

Loretta: Man, I gotta get me a couple.

Jeremy: You know what pissed me off though? She actually asked me to ask Elaine to stay home.

Loretta: Get out!

Jeremy: I couldn't believe it! She went off on this whole family thing, "it's a family crisis and I need my family to help me!" This is gonna be one hell of a pleasant ride, huh?

Loretta: You can say that again.

Jeremy: Hey, can I count on you to help me with our stuff?

Loretta: What? Do I look like Two Guys and a Truck? All I've done since I got here is move crap.

Jeremy: Come on, pregnant women don't seem to travel too lightly.

Loretta: So stop getting her knocked up! *Exits to Kitchen* Hey Rach, Fertile Man is here!

Rachael: Oh good! Lo, Honey, do me a favor, put the rolls in the oven, it's all set, you don't have to change the temperature or anything else. Just put the rolls in the oven. They are already on a cookie sheet. And watch them so that they don't burn ... you don't have to do anything else, everything else should be all set. Just the rolls. Can you do that please, Lo?

Loretta: You want me to do what with the what? The chicken ... the rice ...450 degrees ...

Rachael: Loretta ...

Loretta: The rolls, jeez, alright ... humor?

Rachael: *Crosses to Jeremy* Oh Jeremy, I am so glad you are here, thank you for coming. I really need your help this weekend. I need someone who is ... well ... normal.

Loretta: Uh, hello! What am I?

Rachael: Loretta, the rolls! But really Jeremy, thank you. I need this.

Jeremy: I'm glad I can help, really. It's never a problem for me to get here, but what is going on? You are being all mysterious and weird Rach, I wish you would tell me what the hell is going on? I didn't drive all this way to play some mystery who dunnit, that's not what this weekend is going to be about, is it?

Rachael: *defensive* OK?

Jeremy: Sorry, I don't mean to be so harsh when I just walked in the door, but what is going on? You've got me a bit worked up, I'm worried.

Rachael: We will discuss everything after dinner, I promise. Let's get through dinner, no arguing, nothing taken the wrong way ...

Jeremy: Fine, you're right, let's just catch up a bit first.

Rachael: And speaking of not taking things the wrong way ... I know that this is going to sound mean, and I truly don't want it to come off that way, I don't. I mean, I really like Elaine, you know that I do ... but I am glad you didn't bring her this trip. It would have been even more difficult than it's already going to be, I think. You know how she can be ... and, well, this is really a family thing ... and ...

Elaine enters

Elaine: And Elaine, not really being a part of the family, just the means to squeeze out subsequent generations since no one else seems to manage to be able to perform that mundane task, well, she would really just be in the way, now wouldn't she?

Loretta: Oops.

Elaine: Hi, Rachael, How are you? I'm just fine, thank you for asking.

Jeremy: Good one Rach ... uh, Elaine ...

Rachael: Oh my God. Elaine, I ... I am so sorry, Elaine. Really I am truly truly sorry, I didn't mean to, well ... it's just ... I've been under a lot of ... oh, I don't know ... This is not going the way I had hoped ... Please just give me a chance and I will be able to explain things better later. After dinner, ok? Please? We'll eat, then we'll talk, and then ... Well, again, I am really sorry. You should have heard me when Loretta got here.

Loretta: Oh yeah! You need to be warned, I'm going to be here, well ... at least I said that I was coming. Who knows if I'll actually show up, I mean, we all know how dependable I am, and, what was it? Uh, God only knows what I might look like this time!

Rachael: Thank you Lo! How are those rolls coming?

Loretta: Oh shit!

Rachael: We'll eat as soon as you get your things put away. I'll make some drinks.

Jeremy and Elaine exit upstairs. Rachael crosses to kitchen. Daddy is heard off stage as lights fade.

Daddy: What the hell is burning?

End scene i

Act I scene ii: The Informing

The setting is the same as before. The time is immediately following dinner. Rachael and Elaine are clearing the dishes, they can be seen as they go in and out of the kitchen. Daddy, Jeremy, and Loretta are sitting around the table talking.

Daddy: I don't know why you can't ever manage to get a date, you sure can cook!

Rachael: Probably because you scare them all away.

Daddy: Jeremy, does uh, Elaine, cook well? You see, I've never had the opportunity to taste any of her cooking. All these years and we never really got to see you all that much, well, your Mother always complained that it was never enough. And when we did see you, you always came to our house, but we never went to yours. Not that I care all that much, mind you ... I mean I always thought her parents were a bit snooty, but still.

Elaine: I think I'm a great cook, thank you for asking!

Jeremy: Oh boy.

Elaine: And you are, and were, always welcome in our home, as I remember it the two of you just chose to do differently ... And as for my parents, well that's kind of funny, because they always thought you were rather crass and disagreeable. *Exits to kitchen*

Daddy: *To Loretta* What the hell is crass?

Jeremy: It's a kinder, gentler way of saying you're an ass.

Loretta: When did Elaine get balls?

Daddy: She's always had'm. Keeps'm in her purse ... with the rest of Jer's genitalia.

Jeremy: You are an ass, Dad. How Rachael can live with you is beyond me.

Daddy: Is that the right word? Genitalia?

Loretta: So Elaine wears the pants?

Jeremy: Not as well as you.

Loretta: Uh, good one Jer.

Daddy: Genitalia ...

Lights fade on table and focus on Rachael and Elaine

Rachel: You are really beginning to handle yourself quite well in this family, I'm impressed ... I never heard you speak up like that before, good for you.

Elaine: Jeremy has always told me not to let him get under my skin, just hit back. He said if I hit back, then things would get easier, I'd get more respect or, I don't know ... so I thought I'd give it a try.

Rachael: And you did ...

Elaine: I was always worried about upsetting things if I did, you know, with your mother and all. Frankly, Jeremy has told me stories, and well, I was never really comfortable. I know you all love each other, but the tension is always a bit high. I'm just not used to that kind of thing, my family is not quite as ...

Rachael: Colorful?

Elaine: Colorful works I suppose ... yeah, colorful ... not to say my family is perfect. I mean we have our issues.

Rachael: All families do.

Elaine: But I guess it's just that we feel ok with our own palette, if we stay with you color analogy.

Rachael: You're probably right.

Elaine: I guess I was just never comfortable, so when things were said or even insinuated ... I always smiled, or walked away, or got my feelings hurt.

Rachael: And now?

Elaine: Now I've got four kids ages 8, 6, 3, 18 months and one well on its way ... I've become desensitized and a bit protective, so don't screw with me or my kids. And definitely not with my hormones going off the way they are right now.

Scene shifts back to table

Jeremy: ... and a couple of guys I have are just, well, they can't do shit. No common sense, no people skills ... they handle the computer stuff just fine, but get them in front of people and ...

Loretta: Gee, Jer, sounds so exciting. How do you do it?

Jeremy: Right, and what is it you do? Wait, oh ... that's right, you do ... nothing!

Daddy: God, I miss the fights!

Loretta: I don't ...

Jeremy: Well, let's see, we don't want to talk about my job, and Lo doesn't do anything to talk about, so what about you, Daddy? I mean, we came here for you and Rach, right? So what's going on Pops?

Loretta: I am back in school, you know. Not that you asked.

Jeremy: Rachael asked us to come here for a reason. I doubt very much that she just missed these delightful family gatherings that we all love so much. So why? Rachael isn't talking, she's playing that mystery game she always plays. She gets us all worked up, usually over nothing, but she won't tell us what it is. Should I be worried? What's going on Dad, what's going on with you, what's with Rach?

Daddy: Rach? What is wrong with Rachael ... now there's a good question. *Thinks for a moment* Lord only knows! You name it, it's wrong ... you'll have to take that up with her.

Loretta: I'm taking psychology.

Jeremy: Well, I've tried and I get nowhere with that one. So I'll try this ... what about you?

Daddy: Me? I've been a little sick. That's all, I'm sick.

Loretta: I might major in it.

Jeremy: How sick?

Daddy: I've been a little sick.

Shift to kitchen

Rachael: Elaine, I just want to say again that I'm sorry about before, I ... I really just try ... well, I'm sorry.

Elaine: Hey, I'm a tough girl, don't worry about me ... I can understand pressure, I can understand stress, and I can take not being liked ...

Rachael: It's not that at all ... Elaine, listen, I do like you. You're my sister-in-law ... you are family. I don't know what makes me act so stupid sometimes. It's the stress I guess, or it's the ... oh I don't know. I sound like I'm making excuses ... it was just mean ... and ...

Elaine: And I told you, I am fine, I don't care. I'm over it. Look, I love Jeremy, I love my children, and I love my family. By extension that means all of you. I don't have to like everything you do ... I don't even have to like all of you ... but I do have to ...

Rachael: Elaine ... thank you. You don't deserve to be in this family ... I mean, this family doesn't deserve to have you. You are really good to us, good for us ... and Jer.

Elaine: He's been pretty good for me too, you know. It works both ways.

Rachael: I think Jeremy may have gotten the better deal.

Elaine: There are days that I would agree.

Rachael: So . . . can you throw some of your hormones towards my sister? Keep her in line?

Elaine: Oh I just might have to. You know, I have a feeling that that girl just may push one or two of my buttons this weekend. So watch out!

Rachael: You just have to make sure that I'm around to see it when you do. Deal?

Elaine: You got it.

Shift to table

Jeremy: A little under the weather, a little lung cancer? What do you mean?

Loretta: I'm also taking a Women's Literature class.

Daddy: Stop your nagging, you sound like a damn woman ... well, you sound like Rachael anyway.

Loretta: I was going to major in that, but there is so much boring crap to read.

Jeremy: God damn it Dad, just give me a straight answer. You know I can't get one from Rachael, she blows everything out of proportion, and...

Loretta: These women are always talking about love, and trees, and crap I just don't get.

Jeremy: Would you shut up! My God! No one cares! Shut up!

Daddy: Jeremy, you shut up! Hey Lo, honey, I care, tell me about them trees. Jeremy, get us a drink.

Shift to kitchen

Rachael: I really didn't expect her to come, I asked, because, well, I thought it was the right thing to do. I mean, she is our sister, she should be involved, but I didn't think she would come. I think she is what has set me off. The anticipation of what she might do, what she might say, how she might react. She is so oblivious and yet so sensitive, I don't understand it. She is unpredictable, that's what it is, and ... and there I go making excuses again. I just can't seem to hold it together.

Elaine: Rachael, you don't need to make any excuses on my account, OK? I understand, I do. And we're fine.

Rachael: Thank you Elaine ... now how about we take out this beautiful, if I do say so myself, coconut cake that I made this morning ... and coffee and let's just move on. My new nephew ...

Elaine: Or niece!

Rachael: Niece? Oh please ... after four boys? I've given up hope. You're having a boy! *Elaine feigns disappointment* OK, the new baby needs some of my coconut cake. I still won't say she.

Elaine: Alright, don't say she, but your favorite sister-in-law has been eyeing this cake since we got here! I am all about this coconut cake!

Lights on both groups

Elaine: *Entering from kitchen carrying cake* Rachael is getting the coffee and I am bringing out the cake ... isn't it gorgeous?

Daddy: She's fucking Betty Crocker.

Jeremy: I thought Lo was?

Loretta: Good looks and witty too? What rock did you find this boy under?

Elaine: Oh please, I never thought he was witty. Just cute. Who wants?

Rachael: *Enters with tray of coffee and necessities* I've got coffee ... and there's tea or milk if any one would rather.

Daddy: I'd rather have a little something else ... and since Jeremy isn't moving, can I interest anyone? Come on, how about it, Lo?

Loretta: Yeah, I could use a nice stiff one.

Jeremy: Now there's a sentence I don't regularly associate with you, sis.

Rachael: Could we at least try to have a talk without the quips and witty repartee?

Loretta: Let's be real here, Jer ... you could mean either of us!

Jeremy: Look at my wife, I think I manage a stiff one every now and then.

Elaine: Jeremy!

Loretta: Ooh! You better watch it, Jer! If you're not careful she's gonna snatch em back into her purse!

Daddy: Ahh! Genitalia!

Rachael: I really can't take it anymore, please!?! Now I know there's a lot of unnecessary tension here, and I know that I am probably partly to blame in some people's minds, but I just want to have some nice family time, or at least pretend to, before we get too out of hand. I just want a break from all of this before we have to start talking seriously. There are a lot of, well, pretty big issues to deal with right now, we have a lot to talk about, we don't need to be at each other's throats.

Loretta: Lighten up, Rach. What's the big deal?

Daddy: Oh ignore her. That's what I try to do.

Rachael: Daddy, you're not helping.

Daddy: You're working yourself up girl. Careful!

Rachael: Daddy, please.

Daddy: You think your Mother died? She didn't, she's right there.

Rachael: Daddy.

Daddy: She's just like her you know, just like your Mother.

Rachael: Alright, Daddy, fine, I'm just like her. You have been saying that quite a bit lately. You keep throwing that out there, "You're just like your Mother, you're just like your Mother!" You of all people should be happy then, you're the one who always came crawling back to her!

Daddy: I rest my case ...

Rachael: What are you doing? Why? Are you trying to hurt me? Make me angry? What?

Daddy: Lo was right, lighten up. Rachael, honey, I don't do the things I do to piss you off.

Rachael: No, Daddy, I will not lighten up, I'm through ...

Daddy: Yep, just like I said ...

Rachael: Just like my Mother, I know. Well, if this is who you were to her, then I have to give her a lot more credit, and sympathy, than I ever did. I don't blame her, not for you anyway.

Elaine: Look ... this really is doing no one any good ...

Loretta: Uh, yeah! Hello! Like me?!? I mean, do you think I like all of this fighting? I never did. Do you think I like people never telling me what's going on? And never asking me how I'm doing? Or how I feel about all of this? You and Rachael in the kitchen and Daddy and Jeremy talking about, I don't know what. You know, a "Hey Lo, how are you doing today, how is everything in your life?" would be nice. I've got problems too you know, not that anyone cares to ever let me talk about them ...

Elaine: *Suddenly laughing* Oh my God, I'm sorry. I'm sorry, Lo.

Loretta: Fuck you, Elaine.

Jeremy: Lo.

Loretta: Ooo, stand up for your woman, Jer.

Elaine: It's ok Jeremy, really. Rachael, how about if I clean up in the kitchen.

Jeremy: Honey, sit back down please. Obviously there is more going on here than anyone cares to tell us, so let's call a truce. I don't believe Rachael called on us because she likes these weekends together.

Loretta: And that's because of me?

Elaine: Oh my God! I don't like these weekends together and I didn't grow up with all of this ... but I'd like to at least try to like it. And I'm sure Rachael would like to as well. But we can't, we just can't with all of this high-school-one-up-manship and melodramatic self pity going on. Can you please just give her, and me for that matter, a break? Give it a rest. Grow up! Let's have that truce and please just shut up.

Daddy: I don't think ...

Elaine: I know. Because if you did, then you would have realized that my little speech was for you too.

Rachael: And if any one has any more inquiries on the subject, please direct them to Elaine.

Jeremy: You're right, sorry …

Loretta: Me too, sorry.

Rachael: Daddy, you need to take your medicine, no cake or coffee for you, you've already overdone it today. I'll get you some milk.

Daddy: There's the overbearing Nazi we all love.

Rachael: Daddy, please … have you been listening … let us not do this …

Daddy: *rises* I'm gonna get changed for bed … Elaine, please forgive me for my being so, what was it you called it … crass? I'm sorry, but you'll have to learn to deal with it. It's not gonna change. I'm old, tired, cranky, and basically an ass-hole, but stick around a little and I might actually grow on you. And believe it or not, I hope I do.

Elaine: *Touched by his apology* Thank you.

Jeremy: Good night Daddy.

Daddy: Did I say I was going to bed? I'm changing … And that speech was for your wife. I think I like her … you can go. Elaine, a big piece if you don't mind, and Lo … put a shot in my joe. Rach, back off.

Daddy exits

Rachael: Well, now that we have all been thoroughly entertained …

Jeremy: Rachael, I've said I was sorry, and so did Lo. Now, I plan to do my part this weekend, but you need to put in a little effort as well. We all do. So do everyone a favor and cut the pained and ever-suffering matriarch crap, we had enough of that with Mom …

Loretta: Why do you guys always bring Mom into these things? Mom's dead, Jer, so leave her out of this. Jesus, she can't exactly fight back now, you know.

Jeremy: Oh believe me, she still gets her digs in.

Rachael: Daddy's dying.

Loretta: What the hell do you mean she still gets her digs in? I don't see how you can talk about her like that? You have a lot of nerve, she never did anything to you, not you, you were always the fuckin' golden boy.

Jeremy: And you were always the baby who needed to be carried, always, everything was for you ... everything was about you ... and you're so friggin' self centered that you still think everything is about you ...

Loretta: Oh please, who's the baby now? Whah! Whah! Mommy paid more attention to the baby. Which is total crap! I lived in your damn shadow!

Jeremy: Bull shit! I worked my ass off for no recognition, while the world got excited every time you took a crap!

Elaine: Oh my God! Did you hear your sister? Jeremy, shut up and listen to her ...

Rachael: It's ok, Elaine. Just ... let them.

Elaine: No, it's not ok, Jeremy stop!

Jeremy: Elaine, back off a minute, this is something you don't understand.

Elaine: You are so right about that, mister. And I don't really care to. But did you hear what your sister just said? Your father is dying!

Jeremy: What are you talking about?

Loretta: Daddy ...

Rachael: Please, listen ... Daddy is dying, he's sick, something with his blood ...

Jeremy: What the hell do you mean something with his blood? What is it? Let's not be vague here Rach ...

Elaine: Jeremy ...

Rachael: He won't tell me anything ... and he won't let the doctors say much ... but ...

Jeremy: Oh, so you just don't know? So Rachael, you call us and tell us we need to come this weekend and you won't tell us why, you make us sit through dinner and wait to find out why, then you tell us that Daddy's dying and you really don't know why, in fact, you really don't know much of anything at all. Well you know what? Find out! Aren't you supposed to take care of everything where he is concerned? Isn't he considered your dependant or something? If he won't tell you, make them tell you. Don't we have rights?

Loretta: Listen to your wife Jer, shut up.

Rachael: I have been trying to get some of the legalities taken care of and fix the situation so that the doctor's do have to talk me, but at the same time I am also trying to give Daddy some respect and at least a little feeling of control over his own life. Some dignity. He is hurting, Jeremy. Not just physically, but emotionally too. It has affected him. All of it. Not just this, but the stuff with Mom and ... and, well, he is asking for things and ...

Jeremy: What do you mean, asking for things?

Rachael: He is very emotional, as you have just seen, and so am I ... and sometimes I am not very good at dealing with it. Or him. I'm sorry. So I needed you all here this weekend, and I didn't know how to tell you. Not over the phone. So I wanted, I needed ... we needed ... this weekend to work through some things ... to discuss some things ...

Elaine: So ... this ... illness, it's terminal?

Rachael: I think so, yeah. I am fighting with Daddy constantly to take his meds, to listen to the doctor, you know, to try to fight this ... I just don't know enough about it. I ask him, he says he's sick. He says he's taking care of it. I ask him what the doctors have to say, and well, you can imagine what he has to say about what the doctors have to say. He is being unreasonable, he's being stubborn and argumentative and ...

Jeremy: He's being Daddy. Sorry Rachael.

Rachael: He's being Daddy. He's punishing me. He's pushing me ... and ... well, I'm about to break ... to snap. I can't do this alone.

Jeremy: Hey, you don't have to do this alone. We're here. We can help sort all of this out.

Elaine: It must be sudden, is it related to the accident?

Loretta: I ... I'm not following. Somebody please tell me what is going on? What are you talking about? What accident?

Rachael: I don't know. I really can't say that it is related to his accident ... I ...

Daddy: *has been listening from the hall and now makes his presence known* Well, I can. You bet your ass it's related.

Rachael: Daddy ...

Daddy: Rachael ... well ... go on with your story.

Rachael: Daddy, you should be in bed.

Daddy: Don't push me outta the room, Rach, so you can put your little twist on things. This is not something you can do your little verbal soft shoe with and try to fix what is so God damn broke it's hopeless.

Jeremy: Hey Dad ...

Daddy: So go on Rachael. Let's hear some truth.

Rachael: Daddy, I ...

Jeremy: It's ok, Rach. Why don't you sit down, Dad, let's talk about all of this ... let's just talk it all out.

Daddy: You look like her too, you know that? Just staring at me like that. You look like her. Loretta honey, Elaine, there was no accident. Not really. That's not the right word.

Loretta: What is going on?

Rachael: Daddy, stop it!

Daddy: Your parents are educated, Elaine, so I'm sure you must be bright too ... what do you call it when a man who is in a lot of pain, is sick, sad, tired, beyond depressed ... and ...

Rachael: Daddy!!!

Daddy: What do you call it when he downs a bottle of booze and half a bottle of his meds? Do you call that an accident? I suppose some people do ... but I'm not some people ... Never mind the cake. I'm going to bed. Loretta, take my old room, I'll be in the den.

End scene ii

Act I scene iii: The Blaming

The scene is the same as before, it is after midnight. Jeremy and Daddy are in the den. Loretta has gone upstairs. Rachael is alone in the living room. Elaine can be seen in the kitchen.

Elaine: The tea is almost ready, what would you like in it?

Rachael: A lump of cyanide.

Elaine: Ooh, can you remind me? Does that go with milk or lemon?

Rachael: Nothing, thank you, I just drink it plain.

Elaine: Ooh, you are a martyr ... I need lots of milk and sugar, I have to have it like dessert. It's funny, I don't really like tea, yet somehow I always feel the need to drink it for some reason. I'm not sure why.

Rachael: I know what you mean. There is something so calming about a hot cup of tea, I guess that's why the British are always so calm.

Elaine: One could also say devoid of emotion.

Rachael: That's exactly what I want to be.

Jeremy enters

Elaine: How is he?

Rachael: You were in there a long time. Is he sleeping?

Jeremy: I think so, yeah.

Rachael: Thank you, I don't know what else to say ... I'm so glad you came, Jeremy. I needed you, I mean ... well ... he won't talk to me. I try, I honestly do. He picks and digs constantly and I guess I do to. He just yells and then I snap back and, well ...

Elaine comes in with the tea

Rachael: Thank you, Elaine.

Elaine: Here you are, honey. It's decaf, not that any of us will be sleeping...

Jeremy: Thanks.

Rachael: But you, he'll talk to you.

Jeremy: Yeah, well, not tonight. We didn't say a word. He didn't. I asked if I could come in, and he just layed there. Pretending to sleep. I came in, and I sat down on the bed next to him. It was so fucking weird. I felt like I was four years old again ... but at the same time I felt like I was with Zach. Zach always wants me to sit with him while he goes to sleep, but he never wants to go to sleep. I don't read to him, I don't talk to him, I just sit. And he, Zach, just pretends to be asleep. But when I get up to leave, he opens his eyes and he looks at me, he doesn't say anything, he just looks, and I sit back down. I remember I used to do that with Daddy too. It was my favorite time with him. Just he and I, I would pretend to sleep, and he would just sit there. Not talking. Just sit there. And when he would get up to leave, all I had to do was look at him, and he would sit back down. I never had to say a word.

Elaine: Sometimes I steal a peek at you and Zach. It makes me cry everytime. Is that what you were doing just now?

Jeremy: Yeah, only ... well ... I remember one night, Daddy was getting up, and I just wasn't ready for him to leave, I wasn't ready to be asleep, I still wanted to feel ... I don't know ... safe I guess ... So I looked up, and he looked at me, and ... and he was crying. He looked so broken, so ... I don't know ... broken. And his eyes, they seemed scared at first, then they sort of relaxed and said thank you. And he sat back down. But I didn't feel safe anymore. After that, I don't think I ever felt safe again.

Elaine: What did you feel?

Jeremy: I felt, I don't know, responsible.

Rachael: *Quietly* Responsible.

Jeremy: Responsible like, well not like I was responsible for his sadness, or his crying or pain or whatever, but like I was responsible for fixing it. I was like six or eight years old and somehow I was there for him. Like we switched places. It was like he stole my safety. He stole it from me. And I always resented him for that. Until Zach. Then I understood, well partly. Because Zach makes me feel safe. But I can't ever let him know, because then ... well ... well maybe then he wouldn't feel safe anymore ... and I couldn't live with that.

Loretta: *From upstairs* Hey Jeremy? Jer?

Jeremy: Anyway, he's asleep now.

Rachael: Are you sure?

Loretta: Jeremy, please come here?

Jeremy: Yeah, this time when I got up, he didn't look at me. I better go see Loretta. *Exiting upstairs* Coming, Lo!

Elaine: Oh boy, can I get you anything else?

Rachael: No, I'm fine. Hey listen, you don't need to stay up and baby-sit me, I'm not trying to kick you out or anything, but if your tired ...

Elaine: I can't sleep, not with Jeremy like this. But I'll tell you what. I do have to pee, this baby really loves to use my bladder as a trampoline. So ... I'm going upstairs, I'm going to change into something more comfortable, if that's possible, maybe even shower ... and give you a little bit of time. When I'm done, I'll think about making us a little breakfast, if you're up to it, join me, we'll talk, if not, I won't push, I won't pry, and I won't be offended.

Rachael: Thank you.

Elaine exits. Rachael sits for a moment then crosses to the hall. Loretta comes downstairs. She crosses to the kitchen looking for Rachael. Rachael enters.

Rachael: Hey Elaine, I was just thinking how nice it would have been to have you for a sister. But you know what? I do.

Loretta: But you know what? I'm not Elaine. And you know what else? You have me for a sister instead. Goodnight. Why did I even bother? *She starts to exit upstairs*

Rachael: Oh, Loretta, that is not what I meant, I'm sorry. Please come back down?!

Loretta: You know, I was trying to apologize to you, and I came down here, and ...

Rachael: And now I'm trying to apologize to you ... please come back down here.

Loretta: *from the landing* Look, I think I should just go. No one wants me here, I screw everything up, and I really just can't take being this way.

Rachael: Being what way?

Loretta: So ... emotional, out of control. I really don't like it.

Rachael: None of us do.

Loretta: See, I should just go!

Rachael: See what?

Loretta: Nobody likes it when I'm out of control.

Rachael: Oh my God, Loretta, I meant that nobody likes to be out of control, I wasn't talking about you. Why do you always have to bring it around to you? You've always been so sensitive, everything I say, everything anybody in this family says ... I just don't understand why?

Loretta: *coming down the stairs* That's just it, I'm not always so sensitive. It's just here. I am sensitive, here.

Rachael: I'm not sure I know what you mean.

Loretta: I get around you guys and I feel ... I don't know, it's like I'm sucked back into being five or something ... whenever I come it's like I have to be cared for.

Rachael: Lo, Sweetie, we don't ...

Loretta: You do too, Rach. People walk on eggshells around me, to protect me.

Rachael: Loretta ...

Loretta: You do ... and ... well it was one thing when Mom was alive. I mean, she was always looking out for us, making things right, or at least seem all right. I would come home after my latest "flop" and she wouldn't make me feel bad about it. She never seemed to judge me.

Rachael: She was always very different with each one of us.

Loretta: I know how you and Jer see her. At least I think I do, but I saw something different. Really, I did. I mean, I know I was a huge disappointment to her, but she never really let on. Every time I came to her, when something was wrong, when I failed something, I broke-up with so and so, I mean, shit, even when I came out ... she was disappointed or worse probably, but then it was like she would reach down into some magic bag and put on this public face, I really liked that public face. It made me feel good, it made me feel safe. But when she died that kind of went away. And now, when I come home, I still fall back into being "the sensitive one", but there's no one here to smooth things over any more. There's no more magic bag. That public face is gone, and so is the safety. All that's left is the disappointment.

Rachael: Wow, Lo, I don't know what to say.

Loretta: That's what Jeremy said.

Rachael: Is that why you wanted Jeremy earlier?

Loretta: Yeah, I wanted to apologize to him too.

Rachael: And what did he say?

Loretta: *Mimicking Jeremy* "Wow, Lo, I don't know what to say." *They both laugh a little uncomfortably* And then he said I should talk to you.

Rachael: I wonder why? Well, I think I know, but the two of you always seemed closer than you and I. Certainly in age, but even as friends. I always felt I was too old to be your friend.

Loretta: That's what I said to Jeremy, I don't mean anything mean by this, but it's kind of hard to talk to you, and ...

Rachael: I see, at least I think I do. You know, Loretta, I feel like I try to smooth things over too, I just don't always do a good job. I mean, my public face isn't nearly as pretty as Mom's. But I try, and then eventually everything comes back to haunt me. So then sometimes, I think, smoothing things over is not necessarily the right thing to do. But ever since Mom died, I've been doing it. I've been doing it damn near everyday. Oh, I don't know, it's all so complicated. You may not realize this, you were a little bit ...

Loretta: I've heard this bit before. I was younger, things were different for you and Jer, up hill in the snow both ways, yada yada ...

Rachael: Do you want me to continue?

Loretta: Sorry, go ahead.

Rachael: Well, yeah, no, I mean you were younger, and I guess things, I don't mean to say they changed but things were a little different for you than they were for Jeremy and me. You talk about her public face, and how safe you felt when she showed it. Believe me, Jeremy and I had that too, and it was a beautiful face and wonderful feeling. But as we got older, we got to see the private one too, and it wasn't always pretty. *Short pause while she thinks* I think maybe she never let you see it, because you never caught her in it. Jeremy and I "caught" her I suppose, a lot of times. I think she felt trapped by us after awhile ... And I've gone off on some tangent here so let me get back to what I was saying, I don't mean this badly, but I guess that what I am saying is that even before she died I was doing it. Smoothing things over. Trying to anyway. For me, Jer, Daddy, and even you. And, believe it or not, sometimes for Mom. Really, I've been in that role my whole life. I'm just not very good at it.

Loretta: Yeah ... I mean, I guess you're right, you do try. But I think maybe you try too hard, it wasn't like Mom ever tried, she just did it. But you're not Mom, and you shouldn't try to be. I don't know, like I said, I just get more sensitive when I get here. And then you try to calm me down, and you leave stuff out. I guess that's what it is, in trying to smooth things over, you don't ever tell me things. And that's when I get mad. Mom used to tell me everything.

Rachael: Oh my God, Loretta, no she did not!

Loretta: Well maybe she didn't, I always thought she did though. I never felt like she was lying. She always told me the truth. It always seemed like she was telling me the truth.

Rachael: Do you think she told you the truth, or do you think she told you what you wanted the truth to be? Or more likely, what she believed the truth should be.

Loretta: I don't understand.

Rachael: I know, but unfortunately, I'm finding out that there is a difference. I've always done it, even as a little girl, I think I get it from her. And even though I am beginning to see the difference, I am still trying to do it. And there are a few people here who resent me for it. Daddy, always tells me I'm just like her.

Loretta: You do kind of look like her pictures. Like this one, behind all of the pillows, weird.

Rachael: Everybody says I look like her, why is that weird?

Loretta: Uh, weird that it's behind some pillows on a couch.

Rachael: *She takes the picture and sets it up with others* Yeah, well, maybe some people do think it's some sort of bad habit or illness, but I don't. I have always tried to tell the truth the way I would like it to be, no, the way that it should be. And I just don't see that as being such a bad thing.

Loretta: Maybe you do try, Rachael, but with you it always seems like it's some kind of a lie. Just a lot of lies.

Rachael: They're not only my lies.

Loretta: What are you talking about?

Rachael: These so called lies, they don't just belong to me.

Loretta: You're losing me, Rach, they are lies, they are not true, they aren't real.

Rachael: Yes, I know that, I do, but you see, the lies, the lies are my truth. Your lies, Daddy's lies, Jer's, mine, and certainly our mother's. Oh Christ, there are so many lies that we live, that I have to live everyday, lies about what truly happens. Or what truly happened. What you did that Daddy can't know, problems Jeremy has had that nobody else can know, and now Daddy's trying to ... well, we all have things that we hide. Things that we are ashamed of, and don't want others to see. So we cover them up, we change them into things we want them to be, we distort or leave out the real things. If we make the important unimportant then what we want to be important can be. The real things that we do and say, the truth about who and what we are, that we can't let other people see, well, people can't live with that. We certainly can't. Not in this family. We've never been able to. And because of that, we have become quite good at the changing and the fixing and interpreting and omitting ... and well, the lying. Oh don't you see that we had to lie so that things fit within our realm of possibility, or our sense of what was right. We had to lie so that we could live with ourselves. And you know what? We're still doing it, and we will keep doing it. People always talk about not being able to live with lies, "I can't live with this lie!" That's just not the way it is, Lo, it's not. It's not the lies we can't live with. It's the truth.

Loretta: Well I think that's just sick, that's a sick way of looking at things.

Rachael: So do I. But you know what else, baby sister? Sick as it is ... it's the truth. *Brief silence* Oh but, we don't need to dwell on all of this, do we? Let's move forward, like we always manage to do. As screwed up as this family is, we always manage to move forward, as a family. And Lo, don't leave. I don't want you to. Believe it or don't, but we need you here. We need our family. Right here. So stay.

Loretta: Why do I feel like we've just had some weird "Whatever Happened to Baby Jane" kind of moment?

Rachael: Oh we used to love all of those old movies, didn't we?

Loretta: Maybe you did, they used to scare the crap outta me and Jer.

Rachael: Oh shut up, you loved them too ... Jeremy was always a wus.

Loretta: He still is. So what do we do now?

Rachael: Well, I don't know about you, but right now, I think that I am going to take a bath. A nice hot bath. And you, you my dear should get some sleep.

Loretta: *As Rachael exits upstairs* Yeah, I know, I am pretty worn out. But I think I'll check out the fridge first.

Loretta crosses to the kitchen as Elaine comes downstairs.

Elaine: Hey Rachael, I lied. I'm going to sit for a moment before I start cooking breakfast. I think my shower exhausted me rather than perked me up. Jer's about to have one now, and when he comes down, I'll start.

Loretta: *From kitchen* Do you find it a little strange that no one in this house seems to ever know who the hell they are talking to?

Elaine: Oh, sorry Loretta, obviously I thought you were Rachael.

Loretta: Obviously.

Elaine: Alrighty then.

Loretta: I'm gonna have a beer, you want?

Elaine: Uh, thank you, no. *starts to leave but changes her mind* But I will have another cup of tea if it is still warm.

Loretta: Oh, another cup of tea. Yeah, how about another cup of tea, and while you're at it, why don't you cut the goody-goody crap?

Elaine: My having another cup of tea has nothing to do with my being "goody-goody".

Loretta: So why don't you join me for a beer?

Elaine: It just so happens that I'm a little pregnant at the moment, perhaps you didn't notice?

Loretta: Uh, yeah, I noticed.

Elaine: Oh, well isn't that surprising? You generally don't notice much of what's going on outside of yourself.

Loretta: So, Elaine, do I really make you that uncomfortable?

Elaine: Excuse me?

Loretta: I said, do I really make you that uncomfortable?

Elaine: Oh, Honey, not even remotely as uncomfortable as I make you. But let's not fight. OK? I really don't have the energy or the inclination to have a fight with you. And to be honest, I don't think you're really mad at me, you just think I'm an easy target. And that is where you would be wrong . . . very wrong. So just drop the aggressive act, OK? I want to sit here, I want to relax just a moment, and I want to work on finding some peace. You are more than welcome to join me if you would like to, but let's just relax, and find some peace.

Loretta: Yeah, in this family? Good luck! Not since Mom died, no way, no how. She kept the peace in this family. She held us together.

Elaine: Ahh, so much for peace.

Loretta: Excuse me?

Elaine: Peace. I was saying my little piece on peace.

Loretta: Right.

Elaine: I was just saying how now it's up to all of us to do it. To keep the peace I mean. You, your sister, my husband, and even me. I am a part of this family you know, and I do care very much. I want to try to keep the peace if I can.

Loretta: News flash, your not Mom, and neither are they.

Elaine: Uh, "news flash", I'm the mother of four young children, I'm not about to take on the mothering of a 27 year old adolescent.

Loretta: Who do you think you are anyway? Adolescent?

Elaine: News flash?

Loretta: OK, OK, so score one for the preggie.

Elaine: I'm not trying to keep score, but thanks, I'll take all the points I can get in this family. *Brief silence* From what I've heard, though, your mother contributed her fair share to the dysfunction ...

Loretta: Oh my God! So Jeremy has you blaming a dead woman too.

Elaine: I'm not blaming anyone. And don't get upset with your brother. What I've learned hasn't only come from him, you know. I hear things from all of you, even you. And I put things together. I am perfectly capable of filling in the gaps on my own. I'm not stupid.

Loretta: Rachael thinks you are.

Elaine: I don't think Rachael thinks I'm stupid. We just don't agree that I can choose to stay home and raise a family despite my college education, she feels women only do that in spite of an education. Besides, outside of our arrival, we've been getting on fairly well.

Loretta: Give it five minutes, it'll change. So what do you feel like you know?!

Elaine: What?

Loretta: You said you weren't stupid, that you could fill in the gaps, read between the lines I guess? So what do you feel like you know about our family?

Elaine: I really don't want to do this, Loretta. Really.

Loretta: No, come on, out with it, what do you know?

Elaine: Well, I know that there is an alcohol problem in this family ...

Loretta: Yeah well, Jer blows it all out of proportion, he blows everything out of proportion. And Rach, she thinks everyone has a drinking problem.

Elaine: Not to put you on the defensive, but ...

Loretta: You are a condescending little, no wait, fat bitch!

Elaine: And you are an alcoholic leach!

Loretta: Fuck you!

Elaine: Fuck you too!

Jeremy: *Rushing downstairs* Hey, hey, hey! What the hell is going on down here?

Loretta: Your wife was trashing our mother.

Elaine: I was not trashing anybody, I simply stated that she was no innocent bystander.

Loretta: You don't "simply state" anything, Elaine.

Elaine: I told you I didn't want this conversation.

Loretta: You started it, all this dysfunction crap, and it's all Mom's fault.

Elaine: Loretta, are you sure you are actually taking this so called psychology class, or are you a case study?

Loretta: Fuck you, Elaine! You weren't even there.

Jeremy: Loretta, you are way out of line! And ...

Loretta: And you were hardly there either!

Jeremy: And you are way too young to remember much of anything anyway.

Loretta: Don't pull the seven years older than me crap. You left, you don't know what went on.

Jeremy: I know a lot more than you'll ever know and I saw a lot more than you ever saw. We just never told you. Rachael and I just never told you.

Loretta: Alright, so tell me now, tell me these secret things that you and Rach supposedly know!

Elaine: Jeremy, let's go upstairs.

Jeremy: Oh no, let's call Rachael down here right now and have ourselves a little pow-wow.

Loretta: Never mind, listen to your wife, Jer.

Jeremy: This was your call, Lo, you said you wanted to know you're going to know. So come on, what's wrong? Let's get it all out in the open. Let's go.

Loretta: I don't care, anyway. It won't be true. You're always bad mouthing her anyway. You and Rachael. You're both liars, fucking liars.

Rachael: *Appearing on the landing* What is going on down there?

Jeremy: Not a whole lot, just a little family get together, you know, like the old days? I was just about to share some old family stories with our baby sister, Lo. I can't seem to find the scrapbook with all the family vacations though, you know where it is?

Elaine: Jeremy, sweetie, I don't think this is the time.

Jeremy: Seriously, Rachael, I think you should join us.

Rachael: Oh God, Jeremy ...

Elaine: Jeremy, now is really not the time for ...

Jeremy: Now is exactly the time. I am so sick of her crap ... no ... I am so sick of her. And Rach, I'm a bit sick of you and yours as well. Now I'm pretty sure you're all sick of me too. So ... now that we are all sick ... how about it Rach? Let's swap some stories.

Rachael: I am going to take a bath, I am going to take a long, hot bath. I can't ...

Jeremy: Come on Rach, Let's do it! It'll be like old times. When we used to compare notes? I've got my take on things, and God knows you always have your little take. So what's the problem? Let's put them together for our poor misinformed, and ever so left out little sister. She needs us.

Loretta: I don't need this!

Jeremy: Oh yes you do.

Rachael: Jeremy, I just had a nice long talk with her, I got her to calm down and ...

Jeremy: Well, Elaine got her all fired up again.

Elaine: Don't you dare drag me into this mess!

Loretta: Well you are in it, you're always saying you're part of the family.

Rachael: Jer, do we have to do this now? Do I have to do this? Because I can't. Not now, please. Haven't we had enough tonight?

Jeremy: If it will shut her up, I think she should know some things. We need to clear up a few discrepancies about dear old Mom.

Loretta: You guys are sick, this was our Mom, why are you doing this?

Rachael: I am not going to do this. I will not do this.

Elaine: Jeremy, I really don't have a good feeling about any of this. Can we please not have this ... *the three siblings are looking at each other and not at Elaine* It seems as though we are going to have this no matter what I think. Can we at least try to do this calmly, please? Sit down, I'll get us some tea. Tea would be nice. It's calming ...

Jeremy: Elaine ...

Elaine: Jeremy ... Loretta, maybe talking quietly will do some good. Everyone will have the chance to get some things out, clean up the misconceptions that we all seem to have, maybe try to get on the same page and turn the focus back to your father ...
Loretta: Fuck you! What do you know? You're not even in this family. So shut up. I don't have any "misconceptions." I like my truth. Isn't that what you said Rach? We create our truth? You said that. Well this is mine and I like it, I need it. And none of you can take it! Leave me alone and keep your truths to yourself, I'm keeping mine.

Jeremy: That was Loretta Porson, ladies and gentleman, singing the "I Just Ai'nt Never Had a Clue Blues" ...

Loretta: God, why ...

Elaine: Not funny, Jeremy.

Jeremy: And now, if we all put our hands together, perhaps the lovely, Rachael Driver will delight us with ...

Rachael: Ok fine, you want it Jeremy? You want my song? Here it is. Here is the little secret I've been holding, the one truth I can't keep anymore, I won't keep anymore. You're trying to throw these little bits of blame on yourselves or at each other. Well it's my turn ... Daddy didn't just try to kill himself, he wanted my help. And he still does.

Jeremy: Oh for Christ's sake Rachael, what are you talking about?

Rachael: He wants me to kill him.

Jeremy: Ok Rachael, you have now sunk to an all time low. You sound like Loretta, this is not about you. You are being ridiculous. Cut the crap.

Rachael: I knew you wouldn't believe me, I knew it. I should not have asked you to come, I should not have asked anybody to come. Why do I even bother? Was I expecting anything different? I should have dealt with this myself, I should have dealt with Daddy, by myself. Just like I always have, always! I always had to, why should it be any different now? Things are just the same, Lo is too stupid to do anything and you are so God damn selfish you always walk away! You turn it into some sick joke about everyone else, and then you walk away!

Jeremy: Alright Rach, you've done it! You want selfish? Take a look at yourself. You always dealt with things ... please, you just got off on wallowing in the self pity and the drama. And I walk away, is that what I do? Well, I don't know that that was always the way it worked, I mean, maybe you think it was, but it is how things are about to work out now.

Elaine: I think I'll get that tea. *she goes into the kitchen but can be seen listening*

Jeremy: I refuse to deal with you anymore, so watch me as I walk away. You're about to snap Rachel, and I'm not gonna watch this time, it's not pretty. In fact it's absolutely pathetic. Dad was right, you are just like her.

Rachael: Ok, fine, you don't believe me? You think I'm just crazy? You think I'm making it all up? Go ask him, go on ... you know he's not asleep, how could he be? He is just lying there listening to us. Like we always had to listen to them. Remember? All this screaming, and blaming, and twisting everything ... doesn't it sound familiar? Jer? Just a little? Isn't this what they did? The only difference is we were scared. He is enjoying this, he loves it.

Jeremy: This is me walking away Rach ... believe me, it will be better if I do ...

Rachael: What's the problem Jeremy? Are you afraid I might be right? Ask him. Go on, ask him.

Jeremy: Come on Elaine, let's get our things.

Rachael: You won't do it. Or maybe you can't do it. Hmm? Is that it? Why not? Because you know what he'll say. Because you know I am right.

Elaine: Rachael, maybe we should ...

Rachael: He will say exactly what I told you, Jeremy. He wants me to kill him. And he will tell you ... that he wants me to kill him ...

Jeremy: And why is that Rachael. Why does he want you to kill him.

Rachael: Because I killed her.

Loretta: What are you guys talking about?

Elaine: Ok, this has gone beyond insanity.

Jeremy: What the hell are you talking about? Killed her who?

Rachael: Nothing, never mind, never mind.

Jeremy: Never mind? My God, Rach! You are a friggin' psychopath! Rach, you can't throw some kind of crap like that at us and then say nothing! What in the hell are you talking about?

Elaine: Jeremy, this is getting a little weird, I think ...

Jeremy: Come on Rach! You pushed us here, Come on!

Rachael: Our Mother, I killed her.

Elaine: Oh my God Rachael, she died of a heart attack ...

Jeremy: You're insane.

Rachael: You are forcing me to do this.

Jeremy: To do what? I am not forcing anything. You, my friend, are nuts! You have lost it. And you have just lost me. I'm gone.

Loretta: Jeremy?

Rachael: God damn it Jeremy, don't you dare walk out on me! Not now. Not after all of this. You pushed me here, I didn't push you. You wanted to talk about it, you are the one who wanted to let it all out. Not me. Because I knew that once I started, I wasn't going to be able to stop. And now you want to walk away from it all, from me, open these wounds that I have, all of this that I went through, by myself because you had to go away to go to college, you had to marry her. You had to have child after child and build a life that was away from here. Well, while you were doing that, while you were away, it didn't stop. Life here, as we knew it, didn't stop. It kept on living. And you think you can waltz in here and demand the truth from me, expect me to fill poor little Loretta in on what she missed out on and not fill you in too? You asked for all of it, Jer, and now that it's not what you want your going to just run away from it again.

Jeremy: Alright, Rach, fine, fine. Fill me in. Just cut out all the crap. We don't need all the little melodramatic embellishments you're so fond of. Skip over the tortured act and spit it out. You've got five minutes, and then I leave.

Rachael: Just ... just let me talk ... let me talk ... The night she died, she came home very drunk.

Jeremy: She was always drunk.

Rachael: She had been "out"... I know, she always went "out".

Loretta: What the Hell does that mean?

Jeremy: Shut up, Lo. Get to the part that we don't know, Rach.

Loretta: No! Tell me. What does that mean?

Jeremy: It means she was out fucking some guy! Other than our father!

Elaine: Jeremy!

Rachael: Let me finish ... so she and Daddy started fighting. Daddy had been alone for hours I guess, when he called me, and he asked me to come over and sit with him. He always called me to come be with him when she would do this. So I said that I would. Only she came back home before I was able to get there and I walked in on them. I don't think they noticed me, and if they did, well they didn't care. They were screaming and yelling, and it was bad. I didn't want to hear it so I went upstairs to my old room. But I could still hear it. He was calling her all kinds of names, and she just laughed and taunted him. She was in rare form. I ... I couldn't take it anymore so I came out onto the landing, trying to think of some way I could interrupt.

Jeremy: Times almost up, Rach.

Elaine: Jeremy, stop, please.

Rachael: Daddy asked her to at least think about us. And she said what did we matter? Jeremy was gone, I was grown, and Lo really wasn't any of his concern. He asked her what she meant by that, and she told him that she couldn't be sure, but it was possible, just possible, that someone else was Lo's father. Well that did it, he snapped. He slapped her ... In all my life I never saw him raise a hand to her, or even one of us, but he hit her. Hard.

Loretta: What are you talking about, will someone please ...

Rachael: Lo, I know that must hit pretty hard, but it is not true, try to separate yourself from that part, it was just something she said, try to put it in perspective ...

Loretta: Perspective?

Rachael: Try. It was Mom, she just said that to get at him. She knew it would hurt so she said it. She always knew the exact, mean thing to say to hurt you, to crush you. Remember Jer? She could just look at you and destroy you? She didn't care if what she said was true, that didn't matter, just so long as it hurt.

Jeremy: I remember.

Elaine: What did she do after he slapped her?

Rachael: She just stood there for a minute. I think she was shocked. Then Daddy told her to get out, he wanted her out, gone. He was going to leave for about an hour, and when he got back, he wanted her gone. And then he walked out.

Loretta: Did she leave?

Jeremy: Obviously she didn't, because Rachael found her at the house.

Rachael: I didn't find her, Jeremy, I told you ... I was there ... I was there ... I am telling you what happened.

Elaine: Go on Rachael.

Rachael: When he walked out, when he actually left, she kind of lost it. I mean like I've never seen before. And, like I said, I don't think she realized that I had come over, that I was there. She started screaming and throwing things, smashing pictures, and then broke down crying. It's almost funny, I don't think she thought he would ever leave. No matter what she did, I think she thought he would stay with her. I think that everything was kind of like a test. I think that is how she knew he loved her, because he stayed through all the awful things she did to him, and to us. And if she kept doing awful things, and if he stayed, well then ...

Jeremy: Get to the point of all of this, Rach.

Rachael: Well, after awhile, I don't know it seemed like awhile, she walked over toward the bar, and she poured herself another drink. She took one sip and sort of coughed, or choked. And then she grabbed at her throat, then her chest. She stumbled toward the phone and fell, knocking it down. She tried to get up, and then ... well that's when she saw me. I tried to move, I wanted to move, I wanted to hide, but I couldn't. She looked right at me, right into my eyes. And I looked into hers. I started down the stairs and she kept looking, her eyes were just staring, staring right at me. They were saying "please, please help me." I reached the bottom of the stairs, I picked up the phone, I kept looking into her eyes, and then suddenly ... suddenly, but slowly, they changed.It was like they shot right through me.They went from saying "help me", to sheer terror, to hate. I looked and they were saying "Oh God how I hate you! How I have always hated you!" And with that I realized that I had hung up the phone. I didn't know that I had done that, I just did, I had hung up the phone and I kept looking into her eyes, searching, hoping that for just a moment they might say, "I'm sorry." But they didn't, they just looked back, and they kept looking back at me until ... well until they didn't. They just didn't look back anymore.

Blackout
End Act I

Act II scene I The Recognition

The setting is the same as before. It is early morning, the sun has not yet come up. We see Loretta asleep on the couch. Elaine is in the kitchen preparing breakfast and setting things out on the table. We hear the faint sound of the television coming from the kitchen. Loretta slowly wakes up.

Loretta: Hey Rach? What are you doing up? And what time is it?

Elaine: Now you're doing it. Good morning, it's about 5:30.

Loretta: Jees, I didn't even know there was a 5:30. Hey, something smells good.

Elaine: I cooked. I always cook when I can't sleep. I've just taken some bread out of the oven, would you like?

Loretta: I can't eat until I've had coffee. I can't think until I've had coffee.

Elaine: Sure, cream and lots of sugar, right?

Loretta: Hey, you're good. How did you know that?

Elaine: It's a gift. And I do the same. Oh, I miss coffee.

Loretta: Miss coffee?

Elaine: Can't do the caffeine?

Loretta: Pregnancy is a real bitch, huh?

Elaine: It has its moments. But in times of stress or early morning ... yeah, I'd say it was a bit overrated. Here's your coffee.

Loretta: Thanks. Is anyone else up yet?

Elaine: Yet? I don't think anyone went to bed last night. You and your father are the only ones who slept, I believe.

Loretta: Oh, yeah ... well where is everyone?

Elaine: Jeremy is outside, he went for a walk, a long walk, and came home maybe an hour ago. I gave him a biscuit and some coffee, and he went back outside to sit. And Rachael is sitting on the floor in the bathroom. I did manage to get her to open the door though. She has a cup of tea and a muffin. I've got quiche in the oven now, a pasta salad for later, I've also made sandwiches, stuffed eggs, and I'm about to start peeling potatoes. So, you ready for anything?

Loretta: Ok, I am slightly overwhelmed by your little domestic explosion in there. Please tell me you're wearing shoes.

Elaine: My feet are not bare.

Loretta: If you're having something, then I will. What ever you have is fine with me.

Elaine: I suppose I could take a little break. My feet are beginning to swell. I'll be having some of that coconut cake. In fact, I'll be having a rather large piece of that coconut cake. But I'd be glad to get you ...

Loretta: Oh Hell yeah, that's what I'm talkin' about. Just bring the whole damn thing and two forks!

Elaine: You got it!

Loretta: I knew there had to be somethin' to like about you.

Elaine: I didn't make it, I'm just eating it. Ooh!

Loretta: What's wrong?

Elaine: It's the baby.

Loretta: Oh my God! What'll I do?

Elaine: No, no, no, it's fine. He's just active. See, he's kicking.

Loretta: It's a boy?

Elaine: What?

Loretta: You just said he, is it a boy? How do you know?

Elaine: Oh my God, I did say he, didn't I? I didn't know before, I mean, well, I was thinking a girl might be nice, but now, I guess somewhere inside I know differently. I should have known, I mean after four boys ... well, he is probably a boy. You wanna feel?

Loretta: Can I?

Elaine: Sure, it's the best way to get to know your new little nephew. And it gets him to know you too.

Loretta: OK, what do I do?

Elaine: Just put your hands here. Push a little, I won't break. Yeah, see he's kicking? Feel that?

Loretta: Ooh, how weird.

Elaine: Talk to him too, he loves to be talked to.

Loretta: Really?

Elaine: Oh yeah. Reading and music, all of it is supposed to be very good for the baby's development.

Loretta: And he can hear?

Elaine: I believe he can tell the difference between people, he always kicks when Jeremy talks, and he just squirms when the kids get going. They put their faces on my belly and just scream.

Loretta: Hey there little one ... are you a little boy or a girl? I bet you're cute! You could be just like me. I'm cute! Would you like that? Are you going to be just like your Aunt Loretta? Actually, I don't recommend it, except for the cute part.

Elaine: He's moving, he can hear you.

Loretta: *After a moment* Elaine, what the Hell is wrong with us? What happened last night, I mean, I know everyone thinks I'm stupid, but really I'm not. I'm confused. I am really confused.

Elaine: I don't know. *Pause* I don't know, I think my take on things may only add to the problem, so I am trying to stay out of it. There is only so much of my, uh, newfound outspokenness that may be tolerated.

Rachael: *Entering from upstairs* Oh come on Elaine. Don't hold back, not on our account. Really, I mean it. I know that this may not be coming across so well, I don't intend to sound bitchy or dramatic, but I am at a complete loss for words, and thoughts, and explanations, and I would sure like to know how you, you know, as an outsider ... how it is that you manage to have some.

Loretta: Want some cake?

Elaine: Rachael, I uh ...

Rachael: Oh, I know, it's called an objective opinion. You have an objective opinion. Well let me hear this objective opinion of yours. Can I? Please? I truly want to hear it.

Elaine: That's what I mean. Rachael, we are all very tired, I don't think we should necessarily get into things right now.

Rachael: Then by all means we won't. I'll go into the kitchen and see about getting some breakfast ready.

Loretta: Don't bother, Elaine made quite the spread.

Rachael: Oh, thank you Elaine. How kind of you to take on the entertaining and hospitality in my house.

Elaine: Rachael, I thought we talked about ...

Rachael: If you'll excuse me, I'm going to my room. I need to get dressed.

Elaine: I didn't mean to ...

Loretta: No one ever does.

Jeremy: *Coming through the kitchen* Did I just hear Our Lady of Martyrdom announce her displeasure and depart?

Rachael: I haven't departed yet, but I will now. Thank you Jeremy. *She exits*

Jeremy: Christ, she's a piece of work.

Elaine: Jeremy, we need to talk about all of this, I'm not so sure I should be here anymore, I'm not wanted, by any one really, and ... well, let's go sit outside and discuss this? Please?

Loretta: Hey guys, don't leave on my account, I'm just eating cake.

Elaine: Please?

Jeremy: Loretta, here's ten bucks, run up to the store and see if they're selling beer yet.

Loretta: What, do you think I am, stupid? They don't start selling til ten.

Jeremy: Here is another fifty, go wait.

Loretta: I'm keeping the change. *She exits*

Jeremy: All right, start.

Elaine: It is not about me starting. And if you think I am going to talk to you while you have that criminalizing tone... I did nothing.

Jeremy: So what do you want? To leave? For us to walk away?

Elaine: Weren't you ready to do that just a few hours ago? What changed?

Jeremy: A lot.

Elaine: What? I hope it wasn't anything that your sister said? If it was, well don't get too comfortable with it, because she can act like that conversation never happened in a heartbeat.

Jeremy: Elaine, it's not Rach. It's ...

Elaine: It's what? Tell me, why should we stay?

Jeremy: Uh, let me think, my father's suffering from some terminal disease and, oh yeah, he may be suicidal. My sister is suffering from some demented state of guilt ridden martyrdom and, oh yeah, she may be homicidal. And my other sister is completely screwed in the head, a total waste, and I can't think of any "idal" words to describe her.

Elaine: Don't play that game with me, Jeremy.

Jeremy: What game?

Elaine: The pseudo-self deprecating humor with the intention of questioning one's intelligence game.

Jeremy: Oh that game.

Elaine: I'm not talking to you. *She starts to exit*

Jeremy: Elaine, come back. *She stops* I'm sorry.

Elaine: Fine.

Jeremy: My point being, and excuse me if any of this comes across as a punch line, but, It seems to me that if I leave, then there's Daddy, Rachael, and Lo left to deal with things. And right now Lo's the most stable of the bunch.

Elaine: Jeremy ...

Jeremy: And she's gonna help how? Did you hear any of what was said last night?

Elaine: Did you? Oh my God, listen to yourself. Remember what you just said about Rachael not two minutes ago? A martyr? And perhaps she's a bit of a ... I don't know ... well ... she is into her dramatics. She likes for things to go wrong. She lives for a crisis any crisis. Don't you think, possibly, that she is blowing the story about your mother just a little out of proportion? That she wants some attention, she creates this misery because she likes the attention?

Jeremy: OK, fine, maybe, maybe ... but what about my father?

Elaine: I don't know ... I think she's making that into more than what it really is ...

Jeremy: He's the one that said it, Elaine! Not Rachael, but Daddy! He stood right there and told YOU! He told YOU that he tried to kill himself. That wasn't Rach.

Elaine: I'm not talking about what your father said. I do believe him. But I also believe that people who want to kill themselves do, and people that don't want to kill themselves only try. He doesn't want to die. He wants help, but he doesn't want to die. There's a difference. What I am talking about is what Rachael told us about your father's illness. Now don't get me wrong, I don't think she has made the entire thing up. And it very well may be that she's right, and he isn't telling her everything, or anything for that matter. God knows, I've seen enough to question telling her anything of real importance. Jeremy, you even said it last night, after dinner, I mean, why doesn't she know anything? That whole business with the doctors, and them not saying anything, I don't know, I think it's sketchy. Jeremy, I do believe that there is a need to talk to your father. But WE need to talk to him, not your sister. We need to hear what he says, because I don't trust her interpretation. But I don't think that right now is the time for that conversation.

Jeremy: You don't trust her.

Elaine: I didn't say that, not exactly, I said I don't trust everything she says. She does tend to get, oh, what is the word?! I can't think of the word. Histrionics is all I can think of. Is that right? She is a bit histrionic. I'm not sure if that's right, it may not be the right word, but you know what I mean.

Jeremy: And you don't think we should stay for my dad.

Elaine: Jeremy, don't try to guilt me into this. I am very uncomfortable, I know when I'm not wanted, and right now, I'm not wanted. And frankly ... well ... all of this stress is really not good for the baby.

Jeremy: Ok, now who's trying to guilt who? Not to mention being a little over dramatic?

Elaine: I mean it Jeremy, I want to go home.

Jeremy: Then go upstairs and pack.

Elaine: And what do you mean by that?

Jeremy: What am I supposed to mean by that?

Elaine: Are you coming? Are you? Jeremy, I shouldn't exactly make a six and a half hour drive on my own!

Jeremy: I will drive you home, you can stay with your Mother so you're not in the house alone, and I will drive back. *Elaine begins to exit* Elaine! What the hell do you want from me?

Elaine: *From the landing* I don't want a thing. You do what you think is right.

Elaine exits and there is a brief moment of Jeremy alone. Daddy enters.

Daddy: Great job, son. I mean it. Keep your woman in her place.

Jeremy: Dad, not right now, please. I'll deal with that later. Can we talk?

Daddy: Alright, now first of all I am sick of all this talking crap. Let's talk. Talk, talk, talk. Why do you people feel like you need to talk about every God damn thing? All you do is talk ... I raised a bunch damn women. And look where it gets ya? Rachael is locked in the bathroom, your wife is pissed as shit at you, and you were a big enough of a dumb ass to give your sister fifty? no sixty bucks! And if you think your gettin' any change back, then you're a bigger...

Jeremy: I don't care about the money.

Daddy: I'm sorry, son, you're right, let's talk. It'll do us some good.

Jeremy: Dad.

Daddy: Do you have any more cash on you? I owe ...

Jeremy: Let's be serious ...

Daddy: No really, I'm serious. I took some money from the grocery jar in the kitchen, Rachael doesn't know. And she is in a mood, so, well...

Jeremy: Dad ...

Daddy: I just don't want anymore yelling.

Jeremy: What do you need ... I have to go upstairs ...

Daddy: I think it was like eighty five bucks, I'm sorry, I just don't have any cash. And you see the mood she's in.

Jeremy: Alright, but then we'll talk? *He exits*

Daddy: Oh sure, we'll talk ... dumb ass.

Loretta enters from kitchen

Loretta: Heya Pops! Look what I was able to score? What I miss?

Daddy: Give me one of them cold ones and I'll tell you.

Loretta: *Crossing back to kitchen* You got it ... hey, wait, do you really think that you should? I mean ...

Daddy: Cut the crap, Lo. I'm sick, I'm not dead, and I'm not gonna be dead anytime real soon, unless you all deprive me of my few essential vices. I'm sick, that's all, sick.

Loretta: Um, Daddy?

Daddy: Listen to me, Loretta. What I got might be treatable, and it might not. Damn doctors won't know til they try. They don't want to give any guarantees or false hopes. So we're gonna try. Buncha sons a bitches, they always say they practice medicine cause they're always learning something new. I say it's cause they never get it right. And as long as they keep practicing on me, they keep getting paid.

Loretta: So what are they going to do?

Daddy: I don't know, damn pills probably. I think they make it up as they go. You know what I always want to try? What if we just practiced paying them?

Loretta: Here's your beer.

Daddy: You always were my favorite.

They sit for a moment

Loretta: Are you scared?

Daddy: Of course.

Loretta: Are you gonna die?

Daddy: Yep, I just don't know when. Could be eight months, could be eight years. Hell, I'm an old man, I don't need that much more time.

Loretta: Daddy ...

Daddy: Don't go reading anything into that, I'm just sayin'. I mean, you could get hit by a bus or drink a bad beer *raises his glass*, anything can happen to any of us. I'm just sayin' that at least I'm old.

Loretta: What about all that stuff about Mom?

Daddy: What about your mother?

Loretta: Well Jeremy said some real shit about her, and then Rachael started going off. You should have heard her.

Daddy: I heard it.

Loretta: Well ...

Daddy: *During this speech, focus should be drawn, either by Daddy moving or with lights, toward the picture of he and his wife* Now you listen to this ... and you listen good young lady. Your mom did have some real problems, she had some problems that were real bad. We weren't always aware of them, she tried to hide them. I think she even managed to hide them from herself. Now I know that sometimes things were pretty hard for you kids, but they were never as hard as they were for your mom. She hurt you all, I know she did. I saw it happen, I did what I could, and that was more than likely not enough. And God knows she hurt me, but you gotta realize, I was no angel either. I was not always nice to your mother, but I loved her. I still do, I still love that woman. And she loved all of you, more than you'll ever know. And with things the way they are for me right now, well, I don't need to think about all that other crap. No. I don't want to. Neither should you.

Loretta: But Rachael and Jeremy said ...

Daddy: I don't give a shit what they said. Buncha whiny ass ... divas.

Loretta: That's a gay word.

Daddy: What?

Loretta: Divas, it's really kind of a gay word.

Daddy: Don't be so smart, I'm talkin' to one ain't I?

Loretta: I'm just sayin' ...

Daddy: And I'm just sayin', smart ass, there were problems ... but they weren't their problems. They just want them to be. They both like to stick their noses in where they don't belong. I've settled what I need to settle, I am where I am with it, and that is where I need to be ... it really is nobody's business but mine. That's why I don't say a word to anybody.

Loretta: So ... what happens now?

Daddy: Well, I'm about to be eighty-five dollars richer. Jeremy and Elaine will be going home today. They'll make it til lunch, maybe an early dinner, but I'll need a few more of these if they do. But before any of that happens, I have a gut feeling that your sister is gonna come down and bitch at us both for the beer.

Enter Rachael

Rachael: Daddy, can you please give me just one ounce of courtesy? My God it's barely even morning!

Loretta: Hey! Back off and blame the dyke, I gave it to him.

Rachael: Loretta, I really don't like it when you speak like that.

Loretta: And I really don't like it when you speak.

Rachael: Loretta ...

Daddy: And I really would like it if you both would both shut your yaps! God stike me for sayin' this ... but this time we all do need to talk. At least before Jer and Elaine leave.

Rachael: Oh, are they leaving? I didn't know.

Daddy: Don't act so surprised, you knew they would leave. And, quite frankly, Jeremy does belong with his wife. And as I recall, you didn't even want Elaine to come. Wasn't there some big argument before they even got here? You, trying to make Jeremy keep his pregnant wife at home with their children because Jeremy needs to be with his family right now. That's not why you wanted her to stay.

Rachael: Oh Daddy, please enlighten me with the true reason as to why I did not want Elaine to come with Jeremy.

Daddy: Because you can't take the competition.

Rachael: Competition, please.

Daddy: I could go through a list of how you might feel she has out-performed you all weekend. But the bottom line is ... she didn't try to do any of those things. That's just her. And you hate that. That's why you have managed to get her to leave, but she still wins. Jeremy's going home with her.

Rachael: Daddy, I did not ask Elaine to leave, if she chooses ...

Daddy: Give it a rest Rachael.

Rachael: Fine, I'll take the blame, I always do. Forgive me for having a moment during this highly stressful weekend of not doing well. I'm trying to get help, but it looks as though I won't be getting any. This is not at all how I planned things, not at all.

Daddy: This is not something that can be planned, Rachael, you can't plan things like that.

Rachael: I'm sorry, but I need plans, I need structure. It is who I am. I just need to learn to be more flexible, I guess. I need to be able to change my plans. Make new ones. And that is what I am going to do.

Loretta: Easy, Rach, you're rambling. You sound like you've snapped.

Rachael: Everyone else can snap, why can't I?

Daddy: It is a whole different story when you snap, Kiddo, and you know it.

Loretta: Since when did you call Rachael, Kiddo?

Daddy: What?

Loretta: Isn't that what you used to call Mom?

Rachael: Loretta, don't look for things when you don't have the capacity to do so.

Loretta: I'm not looking for anything, it's just weird.

Enter Jeremy

Jeremy: Hey, great, everyone's here. Listen ... Elaine is not feeling very well, the baby and all. It's really nothing serious, he's just acting up and we'd both feel more comfortable if we were home. In case he decides to drop in early on us. So, we are gonna head back a little early. Today in fact.

Rachael: Oh, well, whatever you and Elaine feel is best.

Jeremy: Well then, I also feel that it would be best if we all went to lunch before we leave. We should go somewhere though, eat out somewhere, try to talk, and settle a few things. I know we aren't going to really settle anything but we can at least make a few short term plans, and be adults. What do you say?

Rachael: Why don't we eat and talk here? Apparently Elaine has cooked everything there is to cook in my kitchen.

Jeremy: Because if we eat out in public, where normal people are, maybe we can avoid nasty little comments like that.

Rachael: I'm not going anywhere.

Daddy: You're going Rachael.

Rachael: Excuse me?

Daddy: I said you're going. And you are going to go with a better attitude, or this whole deal is off.

Jeremy: What deal?

Daddy: Did you get that thing for me?

Rachael: What thing?

Jeremy: Oh yeah, here Dad. It's nothing. Zach wanted Dad to have something ...

End Act II scene i

Act II scene ii The Departure

The scene is the same as before, it is early afternoon. Rachael is in the kitchen, Loretta is on the couch, Jeremy is coming down the stairs with luggage.

Jeremy: Christ, why do pregnant women have to carry so much stuff?

Loretta: We've been through this haven't we, big guy?

Jeremy: Can you give me a hand?

Loretta: Yeah, you know this territory is way too familiar. Tell ya what, brother of mine, I'll go and grab a couple of beers.

Jeremy: I don't need a beer, Lo, I've gotta drive six and a half hours.

Loretta: Who said anything about you? You've got to realize that everything is not about you.

Elaine: *From upstairs* I'm almost done with the bathroom stuff! And I think you can take my shoe bag!

Jeremy: *Exiting* Got it!

Loretta: *Entering kitchen* Oh my God Rach, you really have snapped! What's with the bottle of booze?

Rachael: It is a peace offering for Daddy. Not you. Hands and lips off of it. And don't say a word, it's a surprise. *Enters living room*

Loretta: *Following her* Oh, it's a surprise. A secret peace offering, huh? So what do I get if I don't tell?

Jeremy enters, crosses upstairs, and returns with more things. He will do this a few times while somewhat involved in the conversation.

Rachael: Remember that game we used to play when I had to watch you?

Loretta: What are you talking about?

Jeremy: Oh my God, are you two talking about ... ? Yeah! I remember! Prisoner of War! We used to play that all the time!

Loretta: Wait, you mean like when Mom and Dad would go out and you would tie me up in the kitchen and leave?

Jeremy: Wasn't that cool?

Loretta: I don't remember you being there.

Rachael: Oh, I used to do it to him too. But he wasn't nearly as much fun as you were, he never cried.

Loretta: I didn't cry.

Rachael: It was always one of my favorite sounds.

Loretta: You're lucky I never told Mom.

Rachael: Where do you think I learned it?

Jeremy: You used to cry? I thought it was a blast!

Loretta: Yeah, well, did she turn on the gas and open the oven? That's what she always did to me. No wonder I'm so screwed up!

Jeremy: I thought we had an electric stove?

Rachael: We did! I always worried about the loss of power I'd feel when she figured that part out. Somehow, it taking twenty years, I don't feel the loss.

Loretta: You guys are sick.

Elaine: *Entering from upstairs* OK, I am all ready. *Stops while still on stairs and turns around* Wait, I should pee one more time.

Rachael: Daddy! Jeremy and Elaine are getting ready to leave!

Daddy: *Entering from den.* Well then why in the Hell is she going back up the stairs?

Jeremy: She has to pee.

Daddy: God damn women.

Rachael: Daddy.

Jeremy: Ok Dad, I'll be back in a few days.

Daddy: Don't hurry.

Jeremy: Come on! You're going to stay with us for a few weeks, we went through this at lunch. Maybe even stay for the birth. We'll see how it goes. But you and Rach definitely need a break. And to be honest, I am looking forward to the time to be with you. I miss you.

Daddy: God damn sissy.

Elaine: *Entering again* And if we have language like that around my children, I'll be using your mouth for a diaper bin.

Daddy: You better be careful, Elaine, you're gonna raise a buncha homos.

Loretta: Hey! I resemble that remark.

Jeremy: See ya Pop! Bye Rach, I um, I feel like I should apologize again, you know? But ...

Rachael: Does it matter? We have both apologized, over and over again. And we both said and felt and ... still feel the way we do. But we will get through this. I think this will work. We all have a plan now.

Jeremy: Yeah, me too. It will. I love you.

Rachael: I love you too.

Jeremy: See ya Lo! When are you headed home?

Loretta: I don't know, I should probably head out with you guys, Rach, you don't need company right now, do you?

Rachael: You do what you need to do, Loretta. You are always welcome.

Loretta: Yeah, I'll be right behind you, Jer. Elaine, sorry I'm a pain in the ass.

Elaine: With my husband around? Please, I hardly noticed. When are you going to come by?

Loretta: Soon, give me a call when the kid comes.

Daddy: You don't want to keep an old guy company?

Loretta: I'll stop by in a few, maybe when Jer gets here again.

Daddy: Elaine, look after them babies, bring em' up right.

Elaine: Yes, I'll see you in a week or so. If there was one good thing to come out of this weekend, at least I can say that I think I understand you a little more. Maybe ...

Jeremy: Alright, Elaine, let's get on the road. We don't want to get home too late. See you in a few.

Elaine: Rachael ...

Rachael: Elaine ... you don't have to ...

Elaine: I would like to think that we are in a place where we can begin again. Maybe appreciate one another, start over ... again.

Rachael: I would too, and I think that we will ... that we are. There will definitely have to be some starting over, but that's good, right? Now, let's not get too serious. Our family moves forward ... remember that. No matter what happens, we always manage to pick up the pieces and move forward. Let's move forward Elaine. We both got our feelings a bit hurt this weekend, but I hold no grudges, I don't. And like Daddy said, you've got the babies to look after, Elaine, you need to take care of your family.

Elaine: Think about coming out when the baby is here.

Rachael: I'll think about it.

Jeremy: Let's go! Good bye!

They all say goodbye as Jeremy and Elaine exit. Daddy watches them leave, we notice he is visibly disturbed. Rachael crosses to the kitchen.

Loretta: So, Dad, is there a game on? Wanna drink?

Daddy: Nah, I'm good.

Loretta: What?

Daddy: What am I sayin'? I mean yeah, I think I will have a drink. I'll take a beer if you don't mind.

Loretta: Oh, I'm not talkin' about a beer, I'm talkin' about a real drink. Hey, Rach! Whatcha got hidden in the kitchen? Any forbidden surprises?

Rachael: Loretta, you're walking on really thin ice. I think it's only fair to warn you that despite all outward appearances, and our recent purge and forgiveness kick, I am not in the mood for you. I am still stretched just a bit too tight. So, Loretta, please, not today, not now. If you're going to stay, and you are more than welcome to …

Loretta: I was just trying to lighten things up. "If" I'm going to stay … please. I can't stay here, but … I can still get home and catch a night out. Sorry, Pop, we'll have to catch a rain check on that drink.

Daddy: You don't have to go.

Loretta: I know, but you and Rach probably do need a little down time. And so do I. I can't sit in all of this.

Rachael: We talked about how things would be hard for awhile, but they would get better. Remember that, Loretta, they will get better?

Loretta: Yeah, OK, I'll be sure to remember that. Now could you stop all of this maternal crap, it's really spooky coming out of you. Sorry, I know you're trying, Rach, and thanks, I mean it. But you know, I think that maybe I do need to do a little growing up. But I need to do it, Rach.

Rachael: Stay for dinner?

Loretta: I can't. I'll just grab a shower and sneak out the back. OK?

Rachael: Things will get better ...

Loretta: I know ... bye. Bye Pop! I'll stop by in a few when Jer comes out.

Daddy: Yeah, great. It was good to see you, Lo. I love you.

Loretta: I love you too, Daddy, thanks.

Loretta exits upstairs

Rachael: Daddy, I ...

Daddy: Please, Rachael, not right now. I can't now. I don't want to anymore.

Rachael: I don't know what you're talking about. *Entering with tray from kitchen* What I am talking about is a peace offering. Like Elaine said, starting over. Starting fresh. A new day, a new plan.

Daddy: I don't want anymore plans.

Rachael: I've always got to have a plan. I need the structure.

Daddy: Damn it, Rachael ... why in the Hell did you ask them all to come here?

Rachael: I just had to ... I had to know.

Daddy: Know what?

Rachael: I had to know.

Daddy: You always make everything so damn mysterious, my God, why can't you be straight forward. Just say it. What do you mean? Just say it.

Rachael: It's usually nothing, Daddy, you know that.

Daddy: What the Hell is this?

Rachael: I told you, a peace offering. I made you a drink. You told me to lighten up, well, I am. Sit down.

Daddy sits, Rachael gives him his drink and sits beside him.

Daddy: Well, for you? This goes beyond lightening up.

Rachael: I promised I would try harder. And I won't go back on a promise. Go ahead ...

Daddy: Rachael ... after seeing them, all of them here, I don't think I want to anymore. I don't think I can.

Rachael: You say that today, you won't say that tomorrow.

Daddy: Rachael ...

Rachael: Tomorrow is always different, Daddy, and you know that.

Daddy: But, Loretta's upstairs.

Rachael: She won't come down.

Daddy: Rachael ...listen to me ...

Rachael: Daddy, you listen to me. You asked me for help, you asked me. I couldn't do it. I didn't have the strength to do it then. And look what happened. You think having everyone here has changed your mind? Maybe, but it will change back. As soon as the pain comes again, it'll change. And you know it will come again. It always comes back. You know that it does.

Daddy: But ...

Rachael: Shhh. Having them here has changed my mind too. They'll be fine. They are fine. They are going to be fine. I know that they will be. So ... I can do this now. I can help you now. But you have to help me. You have to let me. I have the strength to help you, but I don't have the strength to fight you. Please ...

Daddy: Are you sure?

Rachael: Please ...

Daddy drinks

Rachael: Is it right?

Daddy: It's strong.

Rachael: Sorry.

Daddy: No, no, no, that's OK by me, I like it that way.

Rachael: I'm glad. *Rachael takes a drink of her own*

Daddy: Rachael ...

Rachael: Daddy ...

Daddy: You didn't?

Rachael: Shh ... just drink. Close your eyes and drink.

Daddy: Lo's upstairs, we could get her ...

Rachael: Do you really want Lo involved? She can't handle this.

Daddy: We could call Jeremy, They can't be far.

Rachael: And then what? Where would you be Daddy? What would happen to you? And me? What do you think would happen to me?

Daddy: Oh God, Rachael, I'm so sorry for everything ...

Rachael: It doesn't matter Daddy, it doesn't. It will all work out now. It will work this time. Everything will be fine. Jeremy and Elaine and the kids, Loretta will make it ... you ... me ... we will be fine.

Daddy: Oh, God damn it, Rachael.

Rachael: Just close your eyes and sleep, Daddy. That's what I'm going to do, sleep.

Daddy nods his head in recognition. Daddy and Rachael watch each other as they finish their drinks and slowly close their eyes. A few moments later Loretta appears from upstairs.

Loretta: Hey guys, I changed my mind. I think I will stay for ... Oh shit. You're asleep. *She crosses to Daddy and Rachael. She smiles at them both and then sees the bottle. She picks up the bottle and turns to leave, stops, kisses Daddy on the forehead and whispers* I love you. *Then turns off the light as she exits.*

Play ends

Last Night
I Flew With Angels

For Four Amazing Women:
Ina, Helen, Jo, and Jane

Last Night I Flew With Angels

Characters:

Esther Jorden: early to mid sixties, reserved, composed, yet un-afraid. She is a cancer survivor, widowed, and self sufficient. She is a retired teacher, volunteering at a hospice facility.

DJ (Darcy Jeanette) Engel: late twenties-early thirties, out-spo-ken, very lively. Cancer victim, divorced, alone.

Setting:

The setting is a park like area on the grounds of a hospice facility. It can be as simplistic or detailed as a designer would like it to be. The essentials are a calm and serene outdoor feel, a fountain, and a bench. The play takes place over several weeks, each scene is a different day.

Act I scene i

Esther appears alone

Esther: Last night I flew with angels. It wasn't the first time. No ... it wasn't the first time. You'll want to know how it happened, I suppose. Well, it's a long story ... no ... no it isn't actually, it's not long at all. It's too short, in fact ... but I'm stalling, aren't I? Well, I was sitting alone, silently ... hesitating, yes, hesitating is the best word. Hesitating as I was about to ... well, as I was about to do nothing, be nothing, I suppose. And that's when the angel appeared. Oh, she was beautiful. The angel spoke to me and lifted me high, so high that I felt there was no longer anything beneath me. And then we stopped. We just stopped, and I felt so warm and so safe, calm, even though I was so high up. And then the angel looked at me, and she smiled. She smiled a long loving smile and said, "It's time," and then she let go. I didn't know what to do, I was so scared, I reached for her, and I could see that she was still smiling ... and I fell. I fell and fell and my arms were reaching for that angel and that angel's smile ... and as I fell ... I was ... suddenly ... surrounded by hundreds, thousands of angels ... whooshing by, pulling me, pushing me, lifting me, touching me, slowing me ... and then ... and then I touched the ground. And then I woke up, and I knew ... I knew so much ... I knew I had flown with the angels. But then I knew that I had always been flying with the angels. I knew that everyday everybody flies with angels. But they don't know it. They don't, no, they won't see them. They won't feel them pushing and pulling, lifting and slowing. They don't see them smile. Oh, God, I want to be pushed. I want to be pulled and lifted. I want to smile! I want to fly! I want to fly again tonight. I want to fly so high that when I fall ... I'll never reach the ground. I'll see that smile, and I won't be afraid, and I'll feel them all around me. I want to fly. Please . . . please just smile.

Lights fade

Act I scene ii

Esther is sitting on a bench, eating a sandwich and reading a book. A young woman approaches, wearing flannel pajama bottoms, a stretched out sweatshirt, and a hat.

DJ: Hi!

Esther: Oh, hello.

DJ: Where'd you get that sandwich? Is there a sandwich wagon around here somewhere? I could really use ...

Esther: Oh, no. Um, I was just taking a little, you know, break.

DJ: Me too. Are you visiting somebody?

Esther: Hmm? Oh, no, I um, I work here ... I ...

DJ: You do huh?

Esther: Well, yes, I ...

DJ: You're new.

Esther: What I mean to say is ...

DJ: Oooh, you're a doctor, aren't you? A lady doctor. You know, I always wanted to be a lady doctor. I never did much in the way of schooling, of course, so I didn't get very far. School was never really my thing, you see ... but to have someone call me Doctor Lady. Oh! That would be great!

Esther: Yes, well, it would be. Only, I'm not a doctor ... I ...

DJ: That's ok, a nurse is good too.

Esther: No, I ...

DJ: You're not an orderly.

Esther: What I meant to say was, I volunteer. I read to patients, I talk to families, I watch their children while they're visiting. That sort of thing.

DJ: Oh.

Esther: Are you visiting with someone?

DJ: Yeah, well ... kind of ... so you're taking a little break. Reading a book. Eating a sandwich.

Esther: Yes. It gets ... well ... a little overwhelming. And you just need to take a break. It is important work, I think, reading to patients and doing, you know, whatever ... comforting them the best you can. Talking to the families. But being around this ... well it makes one ... I don't know ... I need to step away sometimes. You know, just eat my lunch, read quietly, and be alone for a little while.

DJ: I'm always alone. I don't like it much. I like to talk to people. You know, just sort of visit with them? I guess you can tell that.

Esther: Oh yes, well, that's wonderful ... for someplace like this. People like to visit, as you say. *Brief silence* I'm sorry. It's just that I'm usually by myself on my lunch break. I step out here because it is so quiet, I suppose. You see ...

DJ: Am I bothering you?

Esther: Um ... no ... not at all ... no.

DJ: I am, I'm bothering you ... I should leave.

Esther: No, please, stay. It's fine to talk with someone who, well, is young. There isn't enough youth here. That sounds odd, it is a hospice center, what do I expect? But even the younger patients are so old looking and feeling ... I just have to get away from them. I don't want to stop what I'm doing, don't get me wrong ... Like I said, I just need a break ... just a few minutes. *Brief silence* I'm Esther, by the way. Esther Jorden.

DJ: I'm Darcy Jeannette. You can call me DJ, though. I don't really like Darcy Jeannette, but it's what I got stuck with.

Esther: Well I think it's a fine name.

DJ: Thanks.

Esther: Yes, well ... would you ...

DJ: I know what you mean about the people here. I mean, their all dying. It's so depressing. They're all depressed, their families are all depressed ... and all they do is sit there, being depressed. It makes me want to scream. I look at them and I just want to scream ... "You are dying! You don't have that much time left! Do something!!" But they don't really let you do that here.

Esther: No, I would imagine not. I suppose you just have to do what I do ... take a break from the patients, read a book, watch the fountain, eat a sandwich ... why don't you join me?

DJ: No.

Esther: Please?

DJ: I don't have a sandwich.

Esther: Well, that's ok, I suppose I could share mine. I'm really not all that hungry and there is plenty . . .

DJ: You say "suppose" a lot.

Esther: I ... what?

DJ: You say "I suppose" ... like a lot!

Esther: Yes, well ...

DJ: It's ok ... you just want to be alone for a bit, I can respect that.

Esther: I don't mind, really.

DJ: No, I'll see you some other time though, ok?

Esther: I'm here three days a week, most weeks. I always come here for lunch. Next time you're out visiting, join me? I mean that.

DJ: Yes ma'am. I'd like that. I'm here most every day now. For awhile anyway ... you know.

Esther: I do. Tell me who you're here with, what room? I'll stop by and see if I can do anything.

DJ: You don't have to do that, you're real busy, I'm sure.

Esther: No, I want to. I'd like to help if I can.

DJ: Uh, well ... ok. Her name is Dorcas, Dorcas Engel. I know, can you believe it? It is the stupidest name ever. What kind of dorkus names her only child Dorcas? Well, it turns out she was named for her Granny. Still, it's a stupid name.

Esther: Well, it is different. I'd call it more of a classical name, for an older generation.

DJ: Well that's real sweet.

Esther: I'll check in on her before I leave this afternoon.

DJ: I'm sure she'll be "resting" as they say, passed out unconscious is what I call it ...

Esther: That's fine, I won't disturb her, I'll just look in, maybe sit for a few minutes ...

DJ: I think she'd be ok with that. *Brief silence* Bye. *DJ starts to exit then stops* Esther's pretty.

DJ exits

Esther: Bye.

Lights fade

Act I scene iii

DJ is sitting by the fountain, floating newspaper boats, and singing quietly to herself. Esther approaches, sees her and stops, decides to turn and leave when ...

DJ: Dorcas is a real piece of work, isn't she?

Esther: I beg your pardon?

DJ: Dorcas. She's a piece of work. I'm guessing by your not wanting to sit down and your near exit and all ... that you looked in on her.

Esther: Yes, I did.

DJ: She looks horrible, doesn't she? I mean, it's a whole different thing looking at someone when they're lying in that bed, no hat on ... in that room. I think it makes them look dead ... don't you think so? You're not allowed to agree are you? It's ok. *big sigh* You should have seen her before, I mean ... she was never real pretty like, but she was so full of life ...

Esther: Why didn't you say something?

DJ: Yeah, well, about that ... you looked like you needed that break from the dying that you were taking. So, I didn't want to ... you know ... impose anymore dying on you at the moment. So I just didn't say nothing. I mean, well ... I did, a lot really. I said a lot, bout near talked your ear off, it's kinda my thing ... but just not ...

Esther: I see. And Darcy Jeannete?

DJ: Ma'am? Oh ... yeah ... well I told you I got stuck with it. And that was the truth. It's the only thing I could think of at the time. Not at the time yesterday, at the time when I had my name changed. See, I had just gotten' a divorce, and well I felt bad enough about myself as it was, and I knew I just couldn't keep going if people were gonna keep calling me Dorcas all the time. So I changed it.

Esther: I'm not following.

DJ: I get that a lot.

Esther: So ... what happened?

DJ: I told you, it was the first name I could think of.

Esther: That's not what I mean.

DJ: Oh, you mean ... yeah that ... well it's a long story.

Esther: Yes, well ...

DJ: *After a brief silence* I should probably excuse myself.

Esther: No, really, please, you um, you don't have to, not on my account.

DJ: Yeah. Well, as we gentile southern women aren't supposed to say, "I need to use the facilities" ...

Esther: I think you mean genteel.

DJ: Isn't that what I said?

Esther: You said gentile. A gentile is ... well it doesn't matter.

DJ: I guess it's the accent ... *laughing* but don't you think I'm gen-tile ... genteel ... whatever?

Esther: I suppose you could be both now couldn't you?

DJ: I should really be heading on back to them facilities. It was real nice meeting you and all. I'll see ya.

Esther: Let me help you back. May I?

DJ: Thank you, no. I'll manage just fine. Thank you. *DJ starts to exit*

Esther: Dorcas is Greek, by the way. I looked it up when I got home, yesterday … after, you know. Anyway, it means gazelle. It's also biblical. Tabitha is the Aramaic translation. It's a nice story, actually. What was it? Dorcas was a woman of many good deeds, she became very ill, and she died. They took her to a room upstairs where she was visited and brought back to life by Peter. According to the New Testament anyway, Acts 9:36-43 … I think those were the verses. I'll have to bring it sometime, show you. Maybe you'll meet me here again?

DJ: Thank you, Esther.

Lights fade

Act I scene iv

Esther and DJ are seated together, sharing sandwiches. There is a moment of shared silence, there is an ease about them.

DJ: They don't like it when I eat egg salad.

Esther: Oh, I'm sorry, I didn't think.

DJ: I love egg salad!!

Esther: Yes, but if it's not good for you …

DJ: Really, when you think about it, what's the harm?

Esther: Well …

DJ: I don't mean to be funny, or make light of it. But oh my gosh! I know why I'm here. I checked myself in. I know I don't have a long time left. And when I do "pass-on" as they say, nobody's gonna say it was the egg salad.

Esther: You checked yourself in?

DJ: MmmHmm

Esther: I know you're divorced …

DJ: It's part of that same long story ...

Esther: That's ok.

DJ: You've got other people to see, there's really not time.

Esther: It's ok.

DJ: No, really ... it's a very long story, and given my condition ... I really don't think there's time. *After a brief pause* I was making a joke.

Esther: Oh, I ...

DJ: I don't believe you like my jokes.

Esther: Does he know?

DJ: That I'm here?

Esther: Sure.

DJ: Oh, I don't know ... I hope not. I couldn't stand it if he did.

Esther: Do you still love him?

DJ: Wow.

Esther: I'm sorry, I'm getting personal.

DJ: Oh, no no no no no. It's alright. It's just that I never really thought about it before, not really, but, yeah, I guess I do. I mean, part of him anyway. I hate him too. He is a terrible person, but it's not his fault. I mean, it is, no one has the right to hurt anybody, but ...

Esther: He hurt you? Was he abusive?

DJ: Let's just say that he'd be real sorry he wasn't the one that killed me.

Esther: Oh ... I'm sorry, I didn't mean to ...

DJ: You must think I'm real sick.

Esther: No, I don't think you're sick at all.

DJ: Well I am, that's why I'm here. *Tries to laugh at the joke then brief silence* Sorry.

Esther: I uh, I have a daughter ... who was in an abusive relationship. He never physically hurt her, but it was abusive all the same.

DJ: *Genuinely excited* You have a daughter? What's her name?

Esther: Leah, and two sons, Gabe and Ben.

DJ: Oh, that's wonderful! I love kids.

Esther: And you?

DJ: *DJ smiles reminiscently* I do, I love kids, I always have ... *again, very genuine* So tell me what happened with Leah?

Esther: Well, he was very controlling, John was his name. He was financially controlling, emotionally controlling, and just so verbally abusive. It started when Leah moved in with him. Oh my, David wasn't too happy about that. Her moving in, we didn't really see the other yet, I suppose.

DJ: Who's David?

Esther: My husband.

DJ: Oh right.

Esther: Well they settled in, but after awhile, it seemed, we didn't see much of John and Leah. It was just Leah, and then we didn't see much of Leah. She always made excuses, about John working, she was tired, they were going out, whatever. But when we did see her, oh, she looked terrible. Thin, tired, and ... well ... sad.

DJ: What was wrong? Did you ever ask?

Esther: We tried to mind our own business for awhile. I mean, it was her life, she wasn't about to listen to her parents on the subject of love ... we knew better than that. You're still young, you can relate to that I'm sure.

DJ: Oh yeah, I can, I remember how all that goes.

Esther: Well, we did end up speaking to the both of them one night, and it was a big mess. We had gone to dinner and for some reason, I don't know why, I just felt like I had to ask if things were ok. And the look on Leah's face was ... well, I can't describe it..

DJ: I can, it was fear, wasn't it?

Esther: Yes, yes I suppose it was. I wished I had never opened my mouth. I tried to change the subject, but it just hung there, I couldn't ...

DJ: No, you had to ask, you had to know.

Esther: Well, John became irate. He accused her of calling us and telling us all sorts of lies about him, and went on and on about how he wasn't the monster she made him out to be, but that she was. She was so moody, drinking all the time. Always sad, always eating, she never took care of herself, how half the time they never went anywhere because he was embarrassed to be seen with her. I was shocked, I couldn't even speak. And Leah, she just cried and begged him to listen to her, that she never said anything. He said he was leaving, she begged him to take her and ...

DJ: And she went with him, didn't she?

Esther: No ... David told him to leave. David calmly stood up, walked over to John and asked him ... no, no I was right the first time ... David told him to leave. And he told him to never come back. He said he would be by their apartment in one week to collect Leah's things, and that John, and all of his belongings were to be gone. John was not to harm, or even touch any of Leah's things. The lease agreement would be handled by David, and John was never to contact Leah, or us, again.

DJ: Wow, like a threat.

Esther: Oh, knowing David, it was no threat.

DJ: Is he in the mafia?

Esther: A Lawyer.

DJ: I see.

Esther: And Leah, well, even though she sees it was for the best ... now ... well ... Leah has never really forgiven me for all of that.

DJ: But why? It wasn't you ... it was David.

Esther: Oh I know ... but Leah was always Daddy's little girl, not Mommy's at all. She could do no wrong ... and well ... it worked both ways. Leah and David, they were inseparable ... from the moment David first held her ... never was a father more proud.

DJ: But she's ok now?

Esther: We talk. She is getting married, next year.

DJ: *Again, very genuine with her excitement* Oh how beautiful!

Esther: Yes, it will be. Michael is his name, and he is wonderful for her, and to her. A doctor no less. I adore him. And Leah? Well, we talk. I'm hoping this will help us heal. With time.

DJ: *Compassionately almost with desperation, she has taken on these people like her own family* Oh me too! I hope you and Leah heal. It's terrible for a man to come between a mother and child.

Esther: Well, it wasn't the man, not really. John was more or less a brick in the great wall of mother daughter divide.

DJ: There were problems before? Between you and Leah I mean.

Esther: You know that thing you said about a long story?

DJ: Oh don't worry about that. Just don't be offended if I don't make it to the end of the story.

Esther: I'll just say that things didn't go well when David died.

DJ: *Genuine with her shock and sadness over this.* Oh no! David died? When?

Esther: *Perhaps slightly taken aback by DJ's intensity here* Oh, it's been a few years, he had cancer ... of course. A long, long battle that we just knew he had won. And then one day, we found out that he hadn't.

DJ: I'm sorry.

Esther: Me too.

Brief silence

DJ: I guess you should be getting to your other people, I don't want to take all of your time.

Esther: Oh, well ...

DJ: You're nice to visit with.

Esther: Thank you ...

DJ: Well I'll just bet that you've got a whole long line of people waiting to talk to you.

Esther: Oh no, it's fine, really, I enjoy talking with you, as well. It's, I don't know ... easy. Although it does seem that I'm the one doing all of the talking, I should be the one listening.

DJ: Hey, come back tomorrow. But not as a volunteer, more as a visitor ... a friend ... I don't get many visitors and, well ...

Esther: Yes, I will.

DJ: And I'll tell you that story, if you're up for it.

Esther: I'd like that. And I'll bring lunch. Any requests?

DJ: Egg salad.

Lights fade

Act I scene v

Esther sits alone, she has laid out a nice picnic lunch. Once she has finished setting everything out, she begins to read. She reads very briefly, then sits by the fountain. She sees the newspaper boat at the bottom of the fountain, picks it up, and, to her amazement, begins to cry.

Esther: *Pulling herself together* Oh God, this is not happening ... Well, Esther, are you really surprised that this has happened? When you let yourself get involved, well, there you are. Leah was right, the boys ... oh this was a mistake. This was a mistake and why am I even doing this? Who did I think I was that I should be able to do this? Oh what is wrong with me ... why am I here ... what is my problem ... really ... did I really think I could ...

DJ: *Slowly entering* You know, if you're gonna talk to yourself, I don't think I can let myself be around you. There are enough crazy people in here already. I don't need to hangout with the ones from the outside.

Esther: You're here.

DJ: Is that ok?

Esther: I just thought ... Oh my God, I'm so glad. *Goes to hug her*

DJ: Whoa, easy girl, it's ok, I'm not going anywhere, well not for a little while.

Esther: Do you know ... I'm sorry.

DJ: No, go ahead. Do I know how long? Is that what you were going to ask?

Esther: I'm ... no ... you don't have to ...

DJ: No, you're fine, I don't mind. But you know how they are here, they don't really like to say anything about that. They like their little secrets.

Esther: Oh, well yes, that's true. Although I don't think it's about keeping secrets, I just think they don't want to make a mistake, you know, give someone false hope, or make families feel like they have more time than they do.

DJ: You know what I think? I think they have a secret pool and they don't want to jinx the odds. *She laughs*

Esther: *With a small laugh* You are truly something else.

DJ: Anyway, I've been here a few weeks. I signed on with them almost a month ago. That sounds so weird, doesn't it? Like I joined the peace-corps or something.

Esther: Well ... I am very glad to see you. Let me help you sit down?

DJ: Sorry I'm late.

Esther: Oh no, that's ok.

DJ: I had a rough night. I'm good now, just tired.

Esther: Would you like to go back and lie down?

DJ: Oh gosh no, no thank you ... I need to be out of that room. I can't take it in there, not right now. I like being out here. I like the fresh air, the warmth. I love this fountain. It's just so dang cold in there all the time, and ... well, the people are nice and all, but ... I like it out here.

Esther: Would you like me to read to you, or get you something, or let you rest ...

DJ: Will you just talk to me?

Esther: Um, yes, of course ... what would you like to talk about?

DJ: It doesn't matter. Just talk to me.

Esther: Ok, umm, let me see ... Oh I know, I spoke with Leah last night.

DJ: Oh good ... what did she say?

Esther: Well she is planning a shopping day for the two of us, next week.

DJ: Oh that's wonderful.

Esther: It is, if it happens.

DJ: Why wouldn't it happen?

Esther: It's nothing, really. Let's have that story you were going to tell me. How about that?

DJ: Oh no, please ... what happened with Leah?

Esther: Well, I told her that I might have to be here ...

DJ: Why? You can take a day off can't you? Or go shopping on a day that you don't come here? You don't have to come everyday.

Esther: Yes, I do.

DJ: But why? You didn't used to.

Esther: I just do. It's silly really, but I do, for me. But that doesn't really seem to matter...and isn't really the point of it all anyway. It's not how much time I spend here, Leah doesn't want me here at all. I suppose she thinks it's a waste of my time, that I'm doing it for all the wrong reasons, that...

DJ: Is she right?

Esther: No.

DJ: It won't bring David back.

Esther: So I've been told ... and ... and I know.

DJ: Then why?

Esther: Leah says it's guilt. Gabe and Ben think I can't let go.

DJ: I think it's cause you're a good person. Like an angel. An angel among men.

Esther: Yes, well ... I think it's penance.

DJ: What do you mean?

Esther: I mean...I don't know what I mean...it is so complicated. I...

DJ: So tell me about it. Maybe I can simplify it. I am a pretty simple person you know, I mean, that's what my husband used to say.

Esther: I'd like to meet that husband of yours.

DJ: Oooh, I wish David could have met Danny! So ... tell me. Tell me what happened, Esther.

Esther: Ok ... David first became sick about fifteen years ago, I guess. We didn't know what it was. Headaches, nosebleeds, and he was always sick. Everything that came around, he got it. Well, he was getting his glasses adjusted one morning, you know, checking the prescription, and this doctor noticed something funny with his eye. That's just what he said, "There is something funny with your eye, I think you should get it checked out."

DJ: And he did?

Esther: We did. A tumor. Small, the size of a tiny pea, behind his right eye.

DJ: So what happened?

Esther: They operated. Removed the tumor. And life went on. Until it started again. So they operated and did nine months worth of radiation. And then two more appeared, another operation, and this time they recommended taking the eye.

DJ: Oh my gosh.

Esther: They took the eye, they did more radiation and a terrible chemo plan for a year. And then they declared him well. Cured. A real survivor.

DJ: And then?

Esther: And then I got sick.

DJ: Oh how awful, it's just like a Lifetime movie.

Esther: *Slight laugh* I guess it does sound a bit like that, doesn't it?

DJ: So you had cancer too?

Esther: I did, but we caught it early. Really it was a swelling on the side of my neck. But oh how I wanted to die. I thought God hated me. First my husband, now me, what had I done? What would I do? I was filled with self pity. But not David. He held my hand, he fought right along with me, well ... he fought for me really, he encouraged me. I had my treatments, a small surgery, I became a little ill from the treatment, nothing like David did, but he never compared the two. He knew I was scared and he stayed by my side, he gave me everything. And then, I became a cancer survivor, just like him.

DJ: Oh it is a Lifetime movie! Two survivors, one love, wow. *Brief silence* Well I guess that gave ya'll something to talk about anyway. Something in common.

Esther: Then one morning, a little more than a year after my bout with things, I came down stairs and David was sitting in his chair, the television was on, but he wasn't watching it. He was sitting, and I can remember it distinctly ... it's almost funny, how clearly I can still see the picture ... the sun light from the window across his face, the dust particles floating like little stars or planets in the warm glow ... and a slow trickle of deep red blood coming from his nose.

DJ: *Genuinely taken aback* No, Oh no.

Esther: He was rushed to the hospital, the doctors came, the children came ... hospice came, and I left. I couldn't do it again. I couldn't be around it, not again. He was in a coma, for three weeks. He never woke up.

DJ: Oh, Esther ... I'm so ... so sorry.

Esther: He died with all of his children right there, right next to him, by his side ...

DJ: Well that's nice ... a real peaceful way to go.

Esther: And with his wife sitting in the hall. He had a beautiful service, my sons supported me and my daughter was cold. It was nearly a year before she and I spoke, and things have been slowly getting ... well, they've been getting less bad, I suppose.

DJ: And so now?

Esther: And now? Well, let's see, now I am here. I am here, I suppose because I wasn't there for David. That's a little too simplistic isn't it? It's not so much that I wasn't there, but because I couldn't be ... I couldn't be there for my husband. I refused to watch my husband die. And I don't apologize for that. Instead, I am here watching strangers die. And I will be here for these ... these random strangers because ... because maybe they are alone. Maybe no one else can be here with them. Maybe his wife cannot be, or will not be there, his children ... for whatever reason ... I will be there, with him, holding his hand. But it's more than that, I think ... yes, much more ... I am there, you see, for her too. I have to be. I am there for the wife who cannot watch her husband die.

Lights fade

Act I scene vi

Esther is wheeling DJ out to the fountain. They both sit for awhile, quietly.

DJ: Thank you.

Esther: Don't be silly. You hate that room. You needed the fresh air.

DJ: Yeah.

Esther: So you had a rough night, I could certainly help, if you'd let me, you know, get cleaned up, get dressed, and bring you out here when you are not able ... when you are too tired to do it for yourself.

DJ: I hate being like this.

Esther: I know.

DJ: No you don't. You don't know. You are a survivor. I am not. I am what Danny always told me I would be ...

Esther: That is not true!

DJ: It is. I'm not ashamed, I know what I am. I am an empty shell of a woman, barren, diseased, weak, and stupid. He knew it, my mamma knew it ... I know it.

Esther: Stop it.

DJ: Hi, I'm Dorcas, do you want to play with me?

Esther: DJ, stop it! Please.

DJ: Sorry.

Esther: *After a brief pause* It's alright.

DJ: No, it isn't alright, nothing is alright ... and I shouldn't take it all out on you.

Esther: You have every right and reason to get angry. And you're not taking it out on me; at least I don't take it that way. I do understand, you know, as well as anyone in my shoes can ... I know that I am a survivor, but I also know the hopelessness I felt when I didn't know that I was going to survive this ... when I thought I would ... And I know what I watched my husband go through ... there are no words to describe ... and then there are the days when I'm not sure I really have survived anything at all ... I still live with it. The fear of it. And ... well ...

DJ: There is no comfort, not really.

Esther: No. *Brief awkward silence* I do know that some people turn to religion. It is a real pillar of strength for many. It can bring a lot of comfort. Are um, are you affiliated with any particular ...

DJ: My mamma was. Baptist. Southern Baptist. She was a big ol' Southern Baptist. She never really went to church though, she just preached a lot.

Esther: Was she not able to go?

DJ: Oh no ... she was able, she just had better things to do then "sit in that room of non-believers and pretenders".

Esther: Oh, I see ... was she sort of hypocritical?

DJ: Mmmmm, I don't know about all that ... I mean, I think that she truly believed all the stuff she preached ... Oh, she meant it alright. And of course, there was her hair.

Esther: Her hair?

DJ: Yeah. She had really good church hair. I mean, she never even had to wear a hat or anything.

Esther: I'm sorry?

DJ: She never had to wear a hat. Her hair? It was big. Real high and full? *Esther shakes her head uncomprehending* Oh boy ... She had what we called big ol'-southern-church-lady hair. You see, all the little old ladies who had good hair ... I mean, you know how some ladies kinda start to go bald ... and without any help from chemo? And then there are the ladies that don't go bald, they have what some people call "good hair." Any way ... the theory is, the bigger and taller you can get your hair, well then the closer you are to God. My mamma's hair ... it was so big, I guess she didn't even need to go to church.

Esther: *Suppressing a little laugh* I see ...

DJ: It probably was for the best, I mean, if you were sitting in the pew behind her you couldn't see nothing no how. But I do remember she used to take my grandmother to church, when she got older anyway, for awhile, they kinda had to stop going. She was something else, Grandma Dorcas. I was named for her, you remember me telling you that? I kind of told you that before, when we first met.

Esther: I remember.

DJ: Yeah, well good ol' Granny Dorcas would always bring these dolls to church, and not only church, but everywhere really, and try to sell them ...

Esther: She would try to sell them at the church?

DJ: Everywhere.

Esther: Oh.

DJ: Yeah ... they were real pretty, real delicate like ... until Dorcas would describe them, and how she made them ... she had this beautiful flower garden, see ... and this big "water feature." Those were her words, apparently, "water feature." And Dorcas LOVED her "water feature". Of course, I loved it too. Mama says I used to always try and go swimming in it when I was little, Mama would yell at me and tell me to get away from that fountain and then Dorcas would just pick me up and wade right on in ... it used to piss Mama off.

Esther: Well, how old were you?

DJ: Oh, I don't know ... maybe three? Anyway ... she made these dolls from the flowers that grew in her garden. She would use bunches of stems and grasses and weave them into arms and legs and sometimes even the bodies ... or use those ... those cat o' nine tails for bodies ... and then she would use the little blossoms of babies breath for hair or veils or clothes even ...

Esther: Oh how interesting, I bet they were lovely.

DJ: She was really quite creative ... they were beautiful and delicate ... and she would always talk about how every part of these dolls were made from flowers ... "even their little tits," she would say ... "I use the curve of rose petals to make their little tits." That's when they asked Mama to stop bringing her to church. It would upset some of the ladies.

Esther: *Laughing a little more* What about you? What do you believe?

DJ: Oh gosh, that's kinda hard to explain. I mean it's sort of changed over time, you know? But I guess you couldn't really call it nothing that specific. I'm not like Baptist, or Church of God or nothing. Nothing regular like that. I don't know, it's just kind of there, you know? My faith ... and what I believe in, I guess ... I mean, mostly it's just faith though. I always like to say, "I'm not a religious person, I'm spiritual." I'm a real spiritual person. *brief pause* How about you? Are you a spiritual person?

Esther: Well, it's like you said ...

DJ: You're more spiritual like too?

Esther: It is a bit hard to explain.

DJ: Yeah...

Esther: Well, I used to be. I used to be religious, very much actually. I used to go to Temple every Friday night and I even went in for some Saturday services. I never missed a Holy Day, and we have a lot of them ...

DJ: Wait, are you Jewish?

Esther: Yes.

DJ: Well I never would have guessed it. Not in a million a years. I mean, you don't look like one.

Esther: *Amused* And what does one look like?

DJ: Well, I don't know exactly, but ... aren't you supposed to wear that doily thingy on the back of your head?

Esther: Doily ... oh ... a yarmulke, no. I mean, some do, the men, but we were Reform, so David and the boys rarely wore them.

DJ: Ohhh ... what's reform mean?

Esther: Well ... how do I explain ... let's say that Reform is a more liberal view of the teachings of God. We kind of put things in context with the time.

DJ: Right. Like Democrats?

Esther: Not exactly, I mean, well, we usually are I suppose, but ... but the point is, I don't really go anymore. Not since David was sick again.

DJ: He took up too much time?

Esther: No, I just stopped believing.

DJ: Oh, how? Why?

Esther: Hmmm, there's a whole long list of answers to that one ... Why. I was angry with God, I was angry with the doctors ... I was angry with David, I was angry with myself. In fact, I was pretty much angry at any and everybody. I didn't believe a true God could do that to people, I didn't believe that a God could allow such suffering. Especially for someone like David. And I didn't find any comfort, in any of it, not anymore ... but honestly ... I guess I just stopped believing ... in anything really. Especially myself.

DJ: You stopped believing in yourself?

Esther: Especially myself.

DJ: Oh Esther, no, I believe in you.

Esther: *Losing composure* Why don't we eat? I'll set us up near the fountain.

DJ: Esther, are you ok?

Esther: Yes, I'm fine ... no ... no, I'm not fine ... but I will be. Why don't we eat? Let's eat and talk about something else. Tell me more about you, tell me that story you were going to tell me.

DJ: Oh, I don't know ...

Esther: Come on, we always talk about me. And I really don't want to do that today. I want to know about you.

DJ: What do you want to know?

Esther: Tell me about your husband? Where is he now? What happened with him? Danny, is it Danny?

DJ: Yes.

Esther: Tell me about Danny.

DJ: Ohhh, Danny! Danny, Danny, Danny ... We were high school sweethearts. Talk about your made for tv drama. You really don't want to hear this.

Esther: I do.

DJ: Why?

Esther: I just do.

DJ: All right, well get ready, cause it's a good one, real tragic ... I think this one should star that, uh, that Tracy Gold or ... or, I know ... this one's even better ... that girl that was in that show "Wings"? Do you remember her? She had that beautiful hair and was in love with one of them brothers? And she used to be real fat, well, on the show ... not in real life ... at least I don't think ... what was her name?

Esther: DJ, you're stalling.

DJ: Oh, all right ... Danny. He was a senior, I was a sophomore, we were real hot and heavy real quick. And it was his senior prom when he convinced me to become a real woman. And I did. He told me he loved me and always would. And we snuck out to his car, and bam. That was that.

Esther: In his car? Well, that's a little cliché, was it at least exciting?

DJ: No, like I said! Bam! And that was that. Three weeks later I found out I was pregnant. Four weeks after that we were married, and four months after that ...

Esther: Wow, it was early.

DJ: She was dead.

Esther: Oh, I ... oh my ... I don't know what to say ... I'm sorry.

DJ: I don't think anyone should ever have to lose their own child, I mean, there's nothing worse. It's just not natural. *She takes a moment* But I was sixteen years old, forced to be a wife and a mother and ... she was gone.

Esther: Why?

DJ: I don't really understand it, not even now. And I certainly didn't then. My body just aborted ... late.

Esther: Oh, DJ, I ...

DJ: Yeah ... it was real hard, especially not understanding ... being so young and all. And then there was that whole question "why" like you were talking about. Why me? Why her?

Esther: I can't even imagine.

DJ: Yeah.

Esther: So what happened? What did you and Danny do?

DJ: Well, Danny and I tried to live together, you know, our love will get us through this, but it wasn't working. He worked at a liquor store, I stayed home. I was almost eighteen when I was pregnant again.

Esther: Were you trying?

DJ: I was ... I think. Yeah, I wanted it. I wanted a baby real bad. So there I was, pregnant, seventeen, and clueless. That's when Danny lost his job. He got caught stealing a little bit of cash. Twenty bucks. He was going to pay it back, he says, but they fired him anyway. But, we got through it. He went back to school, became a real estate guy and I worked as a waitress while he was in school.

Esther: And the baby?

DJ: It was the third month ... and I miscarried. But I was ok. I wasn't ready I told myself. But Danny wasn't happy. He wanted him so badly. So we tried again. We tried and tried for over a year ... now I have to say that this time around it was a little more fun, he was better by now than he was in the car. Much better! But ... after a year of trying we discovered that I apparently had an issue.

Esther: An issue?

DJ: That's what they say ... what they called it, an issue.

Esther: With carrying a baby?

DJ: Yeah ... my body wouldn't carry them. Like I said, I still don't understand really, the reason why, it was just that at some point in time during the pregnancy, my body would abort the baby. My body just "instinctively miscarries" is one thing the doctor said. Danny was crushed.

Esther: I'm sure you both were. That must have been devastating.

DJ: Yeah, he uh, he beat me up for the first time that night we found out.

Esther: What?

DJ: Well, not too bad. Just enough to give me a few bruises. He didn't understand how it could be my body's fault and not mine too.

Esther: It wasn't your fault.

DJ: I know that ... now ... sometimes.

Esther: It wasn't your fault.

DJ: Yeah, well, it sure helps to hear that ... anyway ...

Esther: Anyway ... so you left him.

DJ: No! I mean, where was I gonna go? I couldn't get a real job, Danny had all the money, and my Mama didn't want me back, that's for sure. Get this, she said God was punishing me, giving me what I deserved for being such a horrible sinner ... and an even worse daughter. Real Christian of her, huh?

Esther: I ...

DJ: So, I stayed. I got pregnant again, and took some sort of drug therapy to try to keep the baby. It didn't work. I lost that one at 14 weeks. And while I was in the hospital recovering, that's when they found it.

Esther: The cancer.

DJ: The cancer ... my left breast. *She sees this is having a huge effect on Esther* Hey, you know what? Why don't we make this a miniseries?

Esther: Do what??

DJ: A miniseries, to be continued, I mean it will have to be real mini and all, you know ... but I just don't feel like talking anymore. Not about that.

Esther: Yeah, it's a lot to take in ... um, can I get you something?

DJ: No.

Esther: Do you want me to take you back?

DJ: No.

Esther: Do you want to talk?

DJ: No.

Esther: Do you want to be alone?

DJ: No.

Esther: DJ, I ...

DJ: I'm sorry, that wasn't very nice, it was a little fun though ... but you know what I want to do? What I really want to do?

Esther: What?

DJ: I want to scream!

Esther: You want to what?

DJ: *Getting up* I want to scream, real loud, I want to yell ... I want to scream, "Fuck the world! I want off!"

Esther: Well ... um, why ...

DJ: I did it once, here, well, not here, but in the cafeteria ... I got up on the table and just screamed ... *she does* FUCK THE WORLD! I WANT OFF! *Then she laughs*

Esther: DJ ...

DJ: Yeah ... they didn't take too kindly to it.

Esther: *Laughing in spite of herself* I can imagine not.

DJ: Scream with me!

Esther: What?

DJ: Come on, right now. Get up and scream with me!

Esther: Oh, no, I ... I ... couldn't.

DJ: Why not? Come on, it feels real good.

Esther: Really, I just can't.

DJ: It's like a big release ...

Esther: I'm really not ...

DJ: It's that word, isn't it.

Esther: I ...

DJ: Yeah, well I guess it is a pretty harsh, I mean ... they even call it the "f" word ... how about screw? Does screw work? Screw the world! No. How about, "F" the world! It doesn't really work. Why don't we just scream?

Esther: DJ, really ...

DJ: *Takes Esther's hand and pulls her onto the wall of the fountain* Come on! We don't gotta say nothing dirty. Just scream ... I mean, we don't even have to say anything ... just scream ... please?

Esther: *With great effort but very weakly she screams*

DJ: *Laughing* Well shoot girl, what do you call that?

Esther: *Laughing too* A scream?

DJ: Oh, you can do better than that ... Come on, we'll do it to-gether, I'll count to three ... one, two, three ... *they both scream, DJ loudly, Esther still feebly but better. Both hug each other laughing. DJ begins to cough and stumbles down into the fountain, Esther grabs her and together the two come completely down into the water. It should not be a big dramatic collapse or fall, more along the lines of DJ stumbling that direction and as Esther helps her to sit they just happen to be in the fountain.*

Esther: DJ ... are you OK ... DJ ... what can I do? Can I get somebody?

DJ: No ... no, I'm OK. I just need to sit. *Still laughing a little* I haven't laughed like that in a long time ... not since forever. *a moment* Oh I'm sorry Esther.

Esther: Don't be silly, what for?

DJ: You're all wet.

Esther: *A little stunned that she finds this amusing* So are you.

DJ: You want to know something else?

Esther: Not if it entails screaming.

DJ: I always wanted to go for a swim in here.

Esther: *While rising* Well you're on your own for this one, I'm probably going to be in trouble for this as it is.

DJ: *Stopping her* Oh, there not gonna fire you or anything like that are they? That would be terrible, I'll tell them it's my fault, that ...

Esther: *Again stunned by her amusement* I volunteer, I don't get paid, they can't exactly fire me ... they could ask me not to come back ... not to play in the fountains with the patients ... but I'll just tell them you fell in and I had to get in to help you out.

DJ: Esther ... can you hold me? *Esther does and DJ begins to cry* Do you believe in angels?

Esther: No. Not really, no.

DJ: Why am I asking you, you don't even believe in yourself ... but I do. I believe in you and I believe in angels.

Esther: I don't see how.

DJ: *After a brief silence* I just do.

Lights fade to black.

End Act I

Act II scene i

Esther is seated by the fountain. She is more at ease than we have seen her. DJ enters.

DJ: What are you doing?

Esther: Oh, DJ, I'm ... just sitting. Waiting.

DJ: Are you gonna go for another swim?

Esther: The last name is Jorden, not Williams ...

DJ: Esther, are you telling a joke?

Esther: Well if you have to ask ...

DJ: Are you OK?

Esther: Yes ... I am ... besides ... I knew you'd be here.

DJ: Wow, now that's a far cry from the last time I was a little late. A few days ago you got all pageant girl on me. Not that I mind a good hug, I mean, I am southern, but holy cow, girl.

Esther: Pageant girl?

DJ: Yeah, you came at me like you was vying for the Ms. Congeniality prize at the Ms. Olustee Festival Pageant!

Esther: *Laughing* The what?

DJ: *Shocked* You never heard of the Ms. Olustee Festival Pageant? Oh my gosh ... it is one of the biggest and most prestigious scholarship pageants in all of Florida ... I mean ... if you win that then you go on to the Ms. Florida Pageant in Orlando and then if you win that ... well, you go all the way on to the Ms. America Scholarship Pageant! It's real big.

Esther: *Still amused* I'm afraid I ...

DJ: But, you know what, as much as I love them...and I do LOVE them...I never really understood why they call it a scholarship pageant? I mean, I respect the girls and all, and they do win money for school or whatever...but you have to wear a swimsuit and an evening gown and have a talent...

Esther: A talent?

DJ: Yes!

Esther: What kind of talent?

DJ: Oooh, and some of those girls are amazing, I mean, it's not just twirling flaming batons anymore...not that that's not impressive, cause it is, especially when they're on roller skates...I mean, have you ever seen anyone do that?

Esther: I ... I can't say that I have.

DJ: Well that's nothing compared to what they have got going on now...I got to see this one girl do this little cheerleading routine, with flips and everything, right before she did a whole gymnastic tumbling run right over to the piano and then she started playing on it...the piano. And then there was this other girl this one time, I called her harp girl, because she plucked the harp, that was her talent...and she was real into it too, and good, law she was good...I mean her head and arms were flying all over the place...she looked kind of like a chicken, I guess that's why she didn't win, but she was real good. I liked her. The best one I ever saw, though, was this one girl...oh my gosh she was beautiful! Long blonde hair, real tan, and bright white teeth...she was just so elegant, she wore this dress for the evening gown competition that was all sparkly light blue, kinda like shiny shaved ice, with this little popped collar...it looked like something Krystle would wear on Dynasty... and she did this one thing in her talent competition, which was dance, she even owned her own dance studio, that's what she was going to use the scholarship money for, going to business school for her dance school business...anyway she did this one thing where she did the Michael Jackson moonwalk while standing on her tippy toes in those ballet pointy shoes all dressed up just like Yankee Doodle Dandy! It was so beautiful, and very patriotic, I just cried and cried!

Esther: I'm not sure if I should be intrigued or frightened.

DJ: Pageants are real big where I come from. I always wanted to be in one ...

Esther: Why weren't you?

DJ: Well, aside from the fact that they don't let knocked up ugly girls participate ...

Esther: You are not ugly.

DJ: Tell that to Danny.

Esther: That's not all I would tell Danny..

DJ: You seem to be in some kind of a mood ... you're all sassy. What's going on?

Esther: What do you mean?

DJ: Oh, I don't know ... you're telling jokes, you're more relaxed, you're even smiling ... I never see you smile. Did anything special happen?

Esther: It's nothing ... nothing much, I just woke up today feeling ... much more ... together, I suppose ... more than I have in a very long time. Almost as though I were at peace with things, it's weird ... but nice.

DJ: Are you smoking something, Esther?

Esther: No, I just woke up feeling peaceful.

DJ: Did you have one of them naughty dreams? Tell me about it ...

Esther: I don't have naughty dreams.

DJ: Oh, I do! You should try it ...

Esther: DJ ...

DJ: What? They're a great stress reliever.

Esther: Yes, well, thank you, but I think I'll pass on that ... I did have a dream though, it was a very quiet ... peaceful dream ... I suppose that could be what has put me in this mood of mine ...

DJ: I love dreams ... I do. I think they can have so much power and meaning behind them.

Esther: Really?

DJ: Oh yes! I had this one aunt, well she was Danny's aunt really, but she used to read dreams. It's true! Every time we saw her she was always asking us about our dreams ... "Tell me about your dreams!" she would say. And then she would sit real close to you, right up in your face, and then she would take hold of your hands and look deep into your eyes, all dramatic like. She said she was reading your soul. And then ... she would stroke your hair, just kinda stroke it with one hand while she was holding your hands with her other hand ... and then she would ask you to talk ... to tell her everything you can remember about your dream ... and then she would just listen. She would sit their listening to you talk, holding your hands and stroking your hair and she would make this low growling noise ... like this *DJ growls* Oh she was good, and she was real creepy. But it was so neat to hear her talk about them dreams ... and then tell you what they meant. Only it was usually something bad though ... that was the thing about it, you felt bad for this, you were guilty about that, you needed to repent for this other something that you did ... I just got so tired of feeling guilty all of the time ... I mean, I started to feel real bad about myself. So I started to make dreams up, just so I wouldn't have to tell her my real ones.

Esther: You made dreams up?

DJ: Oh yeah, and I got real good at it too, I'd fill them up with stuff like ... walking down long halls, lots of fog or spiders crawling everywhere ... a lot of water with a light in the distance ... and this one really drove her crazy ... let me think ... *she gets "into it"* OK, so there's this smiley face man, and he is always hiding, well not so much hiding as he's ... hidden, I guess, behind this huge dark door. And deep inside, on the other side of the door, is nothing but all this blackness ... and when the man opens the door, he opens real slowly and the blackness just spills into the room ... like the opposite of light, you know how you can get like a shaft of light coming into a dark room, it was like that ... only opposite ... and he's always looking at me ... with these eyes, I can't always see them, but I know they are there, just staring at me ... or through me ... and then he laughs. It's this low, deep laugh that penetrates you, right into your bones, your heart, your lungs, you just feel it deep inside of you and then he starts talking to me, but not with words, it's always through my mind, I always just hear him in my mind, like he's there, like he got in through his laugh ... and he tells me how he is going to hurt everyone I love, how he's going to take them from me, one by one ... like the way they took me from him ... like the way he's been taking ... anyway, she went right on interpreting them dreams. And started predicting things like "losing something precious" and that I was "slowly being eaten away by sickness"... well, after awhile, you can imagine ... I started to believe her. I mean, it got real spooky, hitting a little too close to home and all. So I started avoiding her at gatherings.

Esther: She sounds a little crazy.

DJ: Oh, well, she was. She was in and out of a home most all of her life.

Esther: Well, I don't really read that much into them, dreams, I just know that this one felt rather nice.

DJ: Oooh, it was naughty.

Esther: Would you be quiet? It was about me and David ... and the kids, thank you very much. We were sitting outside and we were all in a row. We were sitting in these ... these Adirondack chairs, and they were painted all different colors. David's was white, mine was a pale, pale blue, Leah's was ... red, orangey red? I don't remember what color the boy's were ... I think, no ... anyway, we were looking out over a calm body of water, huge white clouds floated above us and they were reflected in the water below us, it was like we were floating between two skies ... I think that maybe David even said something like that ... yes, I believe he did ... and I remember that there were some young children playing somewhere nearby. We couldn't see them, but we could hear them ... they were laughing ... and David turned and looked at me. He was smiling. I looked back at him and his eyes just made me feel so warm ... and his smile ... it was pure love, so calming ... and he reached over and took my hand in his ...

DJ: *tearing up* That is so beautiful, what happened next?

Esther: Nothing, nothing happened, we just sat there, quietly, listening to the children. And when I woke up? I felt ... I felt nice. *Esther is smiling*

DJ: You have a beautiful smile.

Esther: *A little uncomfortable with her openness* Thank you.

Lights fade

Act II scene ii

Esther and DJ sit by the fountain.
Esther is eating a sandwich, DJ is not.

DJ: I guess I'm just not all that hungry.

Esther: It's ok ... you don't have to eat.

DJ: My mama always told me it was rude not to eat what your hostess had to offer.

Esther: Well, I'm your friend, not your hostess ... where is your mother?

DJ: I don't know ...

Esther: You don't know where she is? I mean, despite everything ... don't you think she would want to know?

DJ: Honestly, I don't really care, not any more ... it's so weird, as a child, I mean when I was one, she was fabulous. She really was. She seemed so devoted. She always made a real big deal out of holidays ... always wanting them to be special. I'll admit that sometimes there seemed to be a little too much pressure around them ... but they were special days. She made them so. But really, it was the day to day stuff that was so great. Helping her cook, I used to love being in the kitchen with her ... When I was a little girl, I used to iron with her.

Esther: Iron?

DJ: Oh yes! I remember one year, I was young, and I usually don't remember things from when I was little, but this ... this I remember ... anyway ... I got this little ironing board and plastic iron, and I would set it up in the kitchen next to my mama and we would both sit there and press clothes and watch our stories. And when I was older she was always there to help me with my homework after school ... and I remember she always made me my favorite snack, it would be waiting for me, right when I got off the bus and came inside, there it was, all laid out on the table ... just waiting for me ...

Esther: What was that?

DJ: Reese's Peanut Butter Cups, right out of the freezer and a Mr. Pibb in a big glass with lots and lots of crushed ice.

Esther: It sounds nice, what a lovely memory ...

DJ: It was, yeah ... it was.

Esther: What happened?

DJ: I grew up ... I guess that's what it was ... I don't know, but somewhere along the line I started to become a real disappointment to her. I think it was like we started to be in some sort of competition, in her mind ...

Esther: Was your father around?

DJ: No, he always traveled ... and then he just stopped coming home at all. She blamed me for that. She said I made him uncomfortable. I didn't know what she meant by that. And for the life of me I still don't. Anyway, she was always trying to be friends with my friends, and then she would get mad whenever I was with them and not her ... and by the time Danny came around ... and well ... the baby and all the rest ... she said that I was doing all of this to get attention. And that it took away from who she was. I was doing this to make her look bad.

Esther: I don't understand ...

DJ: I know ... I'm trying to simplify it I guess, it's one of those things that when you explain it ... well it doesn't seem as bad as it really was ... you know ... as when you were living it ... I mean, the pressure and all. The constant failing, and her telling me how horrible I was, I wasn't a good girl, I was going to hell. One time she told me that she realized she couldn't really love a person who was like me, because that would be accepting my sins. Isn't that crazy?

Esther: Was she? I mean really, was she crazy?

DJ: At this point ... would it really make a difference? I mean, I don't forgive her. I just can't. I mean, a mother is supposed to love you no matter what, and sacrifice ... and do so willingly, so that it's like it's not a sacrifice to do it, you know? I mean ... I would have done that for any of my children, for all of my children, if I had the chance ... she only had me ... but she came first. I love her, I do, it's weird to say it ... but no, I don't forgive her.

Esther: Well who says you have to?

DJ: Yeah, but I do find it a little odd somehow ... that I can forgive Danny, but I can't forgive my own mother. Maybe because she never said she was sorry.

Esther: I'm sorry ...

DJ: Yeah, well I try not to think about her, and when I do ... I try not to think about that.

Esther: What do you think about?

DJ: Well, I think about her hair ... I think about pressing clothes. Yeah, I remember as a little girl I used to love to sit with her while she pressed clothes. I told you that, just now, and how one year I even got my own little ironing board and iron and we would press clothes together and watch our stories . . . oh, and of course there's the peanut butter cups and Mr. Pibb . . . and I remember all the stories she would tell me about my grandmother ... you know, the Dorcas I was named for?

Esther: The one who made dolls?

DJ: With the rose petal tits!

Esther: Right.

DJ: Well, apparently she was a real hot ticket in her day.

Esther: Apparently.

DJ: Oh, but there is this one story Mama would always tell me, and I feel like I almost remember. I mean, I'm sure it's because I heard the story so many times, and it is so sweet. But I do, I swear, I do remember parts of it ... anyway ... she used to break me out of daycare, Dorcas did. She would pick me up early, and we would drive home. She drove this enormous pale yellow El Dorado Cadillac, with a white top and the fin cover things by the tail lights were missing, white pleather interior ... I remember sitting in the back seat like it was a big sofa! But, on the way home we would always go across this one bridge. We lived sort of near the coast, and there were all these saltwater creeks and marshes ... well, whenever we crossed this one bridge on our way home she would always say to me, smiling in her rear view mirror, "DJ, honey, tide in or tide out?" And if I didn't answer her, well she knew, she knew I was having a difficult time at home, and then we would drive right past the turn to my house and we would go and get McDonaldland French Fries.

Esther: Did you ever answer her?

DJ: Oh yeah, and we would still get the French Fries, but...I don't know...

Esther: It is a great story, DJ, I know she must have loved you very much.

DJ: I do remember that ... I think.

Esther: What ever happened to her?

DJ: She died, when I was like, eight or nine ... I don't really remember it, or how old I was, I might have been even younger. I just remember lots of dark clothes and big hair and rain. You know, I don't remember a lot of things, from when I was young. It's weird, but there are so many things I just can't seem to remember. *Brief Silence* Have you had any more dreams lately, Esther?

Esther: I did actually, very similar to the last one I told you about, only this time it was just David and me. The young kids were still in the background, I think, yes, I think we could still hear them laughing. But Leah and the boys weren't there. But not in a bad way, not in a bad way at all, it was just me and my husband. Just me and David, floating between the two skies...

DJ: That's nice. I had a dream too ...

Esther: Did you?

DJ: I did. Only, I've had this dream before. In fact, it's the same dream I dream almost every night now. Sometimes, I lie there and I can't sleep, just hoping to have this dream.

Esther: *She smiles* Now yours isn't one of those naughty dreams you were talking about, I hope ... I'm not so sure that I want to hear about any of that ...

DJ: I love your smile. And, no ... I'm all alone ... and I'm just sitting somewhere, I can't really tell where, when all of a sudden the most beautiful angel appears right in front of me, and she looks at me with her beautiful angel face and she smiles. Oh that smile, it seems to fill me with ... well ... it fills me. She takes both my hands in hers and she begins to lift me, and it's like she is taking me somewhere, she speaks to me and I follow her up and up, floating higher and higher, hoping for ... something. Something I can't seem to remember ... and then she lets go of me ... and I fall, and I don't want to. I want her ... I need her to take me the rest of the way to wherever we're going ... I'm falling and I'm scared, but I can still see her, above me. She is still looking down on me, and when I look back I can still feel her warmth filling me ... and then I feel ... well it's like this warmth is all around me, it surrounds me, pushing me and pulling me all over, I start to become frightened but then I realize it's only angels ... and then I realize how weird it sounds to think it's only angels. But there they are, lots of them, swirling around me, filling me up and slowing me down until I finally touch the ground. And then I can't see them anymore, I can't feel them, I'm no longer full ... and I'm crying. I reach my arms up, as high as I can, and I try to smile! I try to smile ... hoping my smile will lift me up, hoping it will fill me up. Hoping it will bring me back into the arms of my angels. My angels ... but I can't ever seem to hold onto them, I can barely even remember them, I never get to see their faces ... I can only remember, just barely, how they made me feel so nice and warm inside. *Brief silence* I'm sorry, Esther, you're not smiling anymore ...

Esther: I ... I'm sorry, I ... I didn't mean to (Brief silence) Are you sure you won't eat? There's sandwiches ... cookies ...

DJ: Whew, I sure did talk a lot today.

Esther: I'm glad.

DJ: Is there an egg salad?

Esther: Of course ...

Lights fade

Act II scene iii

Esther sits at the fountain. She has lunch spread out before her. She sits alone for a moment. Lights fade

Act II scene iv

DJ sits by the fountain, playing with newspaper boats, Esther enters.

Esther: You gave me quite a scare yesterday.

DJ: I'm sorry. I just wasn't up to it. I'm real sorry.

Esther: Don't be, we all have our off days. *an awkward pause* I was just worried that they might have cancelled the miniseries.

DJ: You're getting better at your jokes ...

Esther: Thanks.

DJ: Have you talked to Leah?

Esther: I did. Yesterday in fact.

DJ: And?

Esther: And?

DJ: How did it go?

Esther: Not so good ... it was after I went to check on you, I went to the nurses station to, you know ...

DJ: And what did they say?

Esther: Well, they seemed a little confused ...

DJ: I imagine so.

Esther: Why?

DJ: Well, it's not like ol' Dorcas gets many visitors.

Esther: Well they said that, but then they also said that they thought you would like it if I sat with you for awhile ... in your room ... and that you would ... well that you would know I was there and it would be of comfort. It made me a little sad.

DJ: Why?

Esther: Well, for starters, because they don't know you ... not like I feel like I do. You don't like that room, you never talk about that room, you like it out here. Why don't they know that? And why don't they know me? I'm here everyday now, to see you ... I volunteer here ... why aren't they ... more involved ... or aware ... I don't know. And I know that they are ... you know, involved. Hospice is such an amazing service ... I just want more for you ... and I know all the families want more for their...

DJ: So what did you do?

Esther: I said, "No thank you," politely, and that we preferred to visit out by the fountain and that I would be back tomorrow morning for my normal work and then I would wait for you by the fountain with our lunch.

DJ: And ... what did you do then?

Esther: Well, I felt a bit rude, because I didn't really give them much of a chance to reply, I just left ... and that's when I called Leah.

DJ: And?

Esther: I told her that my day had ended earlier than expected ... and did she want to meet for a late lunch ... or shopping ... and she told me, "No thank you."

DJ: I'm sorry.

Esther: Yes, I am too ... she was kind of cold with it. And I suppose I know why, I just ... there are times when I wish that I could explain everything to her, you know, apologize to her, for what I was unable to do ... and just reach out to her for ... I don't know ... help?

DJ: Why don't you?

Esther: I wish I could, I do ... but I can't. And I don't know why. *Brief silence* Leah says you have become an obsession with me, you know. She accuses me of ... well ... she seems to think that I don't realize that there really is no ...

DJ: Hope?

Esther: Yes ... I suppose that's the right word.

DJ: Oh, but there is hope, Esther, there always is ...

Esther: I don't know how you can say that? I mean, I've seen this before. I watched my husband go through this ... twice. And, you know ... the first time ... the first time I had hope, I did ... I even held on through my own illness because ... because of David, I was able to have hope. David gave me hope ... and then ... and then when he got sick again and I lost him all over again. I lost my husband twice, DJ.

DJ: I know.

Esther: Do you? *thinking a moment* I thought I had lost David with his first round of cancer. I went through all of the hurt and fear and pain and loss just as though I had really lost him, because I thought I had ... or would ... and then when I got sick, I went through it all again. I was so scared. I didn't want to die ... I didn't want to die and leave my husband and my children behind. I was so afraid of dying and being all alone, and I knew, I just knew that I was going to.

DJ: But, Esther, you're not ...

Esther: And by the time I lost my husband, by the time I truly lost David ... it was as though he was already gone. My children too. It's almost funny ... I realize now that it was me who was really gone ... I still am ... I am the one that's "lost". And I don't really know when that happened, or even how it happened ... and I'm just trying to understand ... I'm trying to find my way back. I am trying, I don't want ...

DJ: And you will, Esther, you already are ...

Esther: No, I don't think so ... I can't do it on my own, and there is no one left to find me, not since David ...

DJ: Esther, there's you ... and your children ...

Esther: Ben and Gabe have their own lives, I mean, you know how boys are ... they just grow up and move on without ever really looking back. And, Leah? Well ... Leah gave up on me a long time ago.

DJ: But you can't give up on her ...

Esther: I have though ... that's a horrible thing for a mother to say.

DJ: *Brief pause* When they discovered the cancer, they took the lump right away. And they wanted me to come back in for radiation. I didn't though, I couldn't face it. It was about three months before I had the ... I don't know what ... courage? But, whatever it was, I came back. And well, when I did, I didn't realize I was pregnant again. They stopped the treatments once they knew, but by the eleventh week, they recommended taking the baby. They said if by some miracle it survived to term, it would have serious complications ... not to mention the serious threat to my life if I tried to carry this baby to term. I told them, "No." But two weeks later I went in, I was in so much pain and I was bleeding and they didn't offer much of a choice this time ... they took the baby. Five months later they took my left breast. I didn't get pregnant after that. Danny wouldn't touch me. Well, except to hit me. Two years later they took my right one. When I got home from the hospital, Danny beat me til I was nearly unconscious, and then he left. This time I knew it was for good. And so ... I called my mama.

Esther: And ...

DJ: And she said she had to go to work and I should call her back when she wasn't so busy and I wasn't being so selfish as to "need" something from her. So I called a cab. I went to the emergency room, they admitted me. I divorced Danny. It took a year, just in case I wanted to change my mind. He never showed up to court.

Esther: Did you ever see him again?

DJ: I got a card from him once ... it came one day around Mother's Day of all times. And he obviously knew where I was because it came right to the nursing facility I was staying at. It said, "Happy Mother's Day, baby killer. I hope you die. Love, Danny." There was a picture of a mama bunny and lots of little baby bunnies on the cover. It was a cute card ... the nurse said so, and then she read it ... it was kinda funny actually, she looked real confused and just put it down.

Esther: This is ...

DJ: Too heavy? Almost unbelievable? Yeah, you should try living it. I joked to one of my nurses once, this one had been with me through a lot of this ... that if they ever made a movie of my life, no one would ever believe it, this much stuff doesn't happen to real people ... that's why it has to be Chrystal Bernard.

Esther: What? Chrsytal what?

DJ: Chrystal Bernard, that girl from Wings. I remembered. Actually I remembered it when I was talking about that dress that yankee doodle girl wore for her evening gown ... but it wasn't the time to bring it up.

Esther: *Slight laugh in spite of her self* Oh.

DJ: I think, honestly speaking, that was the day I discovered it was almost over. Pretty soon I was here, and every day I know, it's almost over.

Esther: You must be scared ...

DJ: Sometimes ... but then ...

Esther: And that is why I have to stay ... I can't leave you, not like this, not right now. DJ, I can't leave you alone.

DJ: But I'm not the one that's alone ... you are.

Esther: How ironic is that? A terminally ill cancer victim with no family is worried about a relatively healthy woman with three children because she's afraid this woman feels alone.

DJ: You do feel alone.

Esther: Alright, so I do ... my children are grown up, they have their own lives, they don't need me anymore ... and, quite frankly they don't need to wait around for me ... I don't blame them.

DJ: But you blame yourself ... Oh, Esther, you have so much to live for, so much David would want you to live for ... instead, you're just waiting around to die.

Esther: DJ, that's just not true ... you sound like Leah ...

DJ: I'm sorry if it sounds mean, but you have got to realize that you have nothing to die for and everything to live for.

Esther: Let's talk about something else.

DJ: There are days, truly there are, when I wish I was in your shoes...

Esther: My shoes ...

DJ: Yes, instead of where I am ... I'm the one who has everything to die for.

Esther: DJ, don't! That's a horrible thing to say ...

DJ: Why? *Brief silence* You said earlier that I must be scared ...

Esther: Aren't you?

DJ: I don't know ... Yes and no, I guess.

Esther: What do you mean?

DJ: I mean, that I know I will be going to a better place, I know that...

Esther: How? How do you know that?

DJ: I just do ... because that's what happens. I have the faith that...

Esther: And what happens when there is none?

DJ: What? Esther?

Esther: Faith. When there is no faith. When you have no faith in anything. What happens then? When you have no faith in anything, what happens to you ... can you tell me that? Can you tell me what happened to David ... what is going to happen to me after I finally die? It's such a silly, useless question, really, I mean ... if I had faith, I'd have the answer, wouldn't I? Since I don't, you think I would know that nothing happens after we die. We just die. And somehow I should be ok with that ... but I'm not ok with that. And I'm left with no ... with no ... no ...

DJ: Hope!

Esther: Hope is as good a word as any I suppose.

DJ: No ... *more of a command or plea* Hope. You have to have hope.

Esther: I told you, I don't believe anymore. I don't have faith in anything anymore.

DJ: I didn't say faith, I said hope. With faith ... how do I say this ... I have faith, because I know it to be true, that when I die I will go to a better place. Now, I don't know for sure what that place will be, but my faith tells me it will be better. My hope gives me the picture of what I dream that place will be.

Esther: And what is it that you hope it will be?

DJ: *A brief silence* I'm not sure I know how to explain it to you. I mean look at me. I don't have much ... like you said, I'm a terminally ill cancer victim with no family ...

Esther: I'm sorry ...

DJ: It's fine, Esther, really it is ... and it's true. I don't have a whole lot. I have my faith, my hope, and my stories. You know, looking back on things ... I'd have to say that was her greatest gift to me, my Mama. She certainly didn't give me much else. But when she was good ... anyway ... she used to tell me this one story about Granny Dorcas, of course ... I mean, how anyone can get through life without a good Dorcas story ...

Esther: I can honestly say that every Dorcas I know has a good story.

DJ: Well, one morning she got up, and apparently she found this baby deer lying in her yard. She thought it was dead, you know, but then she went out and looked at it, and she told it to get up, that's what she did, she said, "Get up, deer, you're not dead"... well lo and behold it did, it got right up. So she started to go back into the house, and that's when the deer followed her ... right into the house.

Esther: What did she do?

DJ: Well, it seems she had this stash of old baby bottles ... seems a little too convenient but that's how Mama always told it ... well she took some of these bottles and she gave the deer some milk.

Esther: Milk.

DJ: Yep! And she fed the little thing baby bottles full of milk, and she started raising it as her own. And then ...

Esther: And then?

DJ: Well, after awhile she started to feed it salad.

Esther: Salad?

DJ: Salad. Well that's what they say. She started with just some lettuce, but soon it was standing right at the dinner table, eating a salad. And it went everywhere with her. She would walk through town, and this deer would just follow her, granted it was on a leash.

Esther: She walked the dear on a leash.

DJ: That's what they say ... my mama says that this little dear of Dorcas' had a rhinestone collar and matching leash ... but the point is, it went with Dorcas everywhere.

Esther: Rhinestone?

DJ: Rhinestone.

Esther: You're making this up.

DJ: May God strike me dead if I tell a lie, not a lot of collateral I know ...

Esther: DJ ...

DJ: And do you know what else?

Esther: I can't even begin to imagine.

DJ: Well ...They say ... that it even slept in the bed with her.

Esther: *Laughing* You are too much, DJ. I don't know how you do it, you always manage to make me laugh.

DJ: And smile ...

Esther: Yes, and smile ... it's been so long, I don't know how, but you bring so much ... I just can't do it on my own.

DJ: Yes you can ... I've seen you ... like when you came that day, after your dream about you and David and your family. You had a smile! That was hope.

Esther: I don't know ...

DJ: My gosh, Esther, like I told you before ... even I hope!

Esther: What do you hope for?

DJ: Well, to start with, I hope everyday that this will be my last day here on God's good Earth ...

Esther: Oh, well I can see how that would bring a smile to your face.

DJ: You don't understand ...

Esther: Yes, DJ, I do.

DJ: No, Esther, you don't. *Slowly, controlling anger* You have your children! You have them, you see them. You love them, you help them, you fight with them, you have all the good and the hurt that comes with having babies, and letting them grow up. I don't!

Esther: I'm sorry, I ...

DJ: But it has been my faith, my faith that my children are somewhere better, that has kept me going as long as I have ...

Esther: DJ, I ...

DJ: And it is my hope ... my hope that I will see them, and finally hold them, that gives me anything at all. It will be just like my dream, I know it will. Only I know where the angels are taking me ... to the arms of my children. And maybe, maybe my children will even be among the angels who lift me up, and carry me away. And this time they won't let go ... and this time I won't let go. And I will fly with them ... like I do in my dreams ... and when they smile, and fill me with that warmth ... I'll be able to smile back.

Esther: Oh, DJ, I wish I could ... I wish I could ...

DJ: Why can't you see it? You have ... you've seen David, he's there, holding your hand, looking at you ... he forgives you, Esther. Why can't you forgive yourself?

Esther: What?

DJ: That's what it is all about ... that's what my angels are waiting for ... for me to show them my hope, my faith, my love ... and my forgiveness. You see, I believe that, well ... that they forgive me for I what have done ... they do ... even the one I gave up, the one the doctors took from me ... but somehow I just can't manage to forgive myself. But every day I try, and every day I hope ... and, Esther, every day that I can smile brings me closer to it. And I know, that one of these days, real soon, someone is going to smile back, and I'll know ... and then I'll be able to ... Oh God, please ... I want to fly tonight ... and I don't want to come back ... please, someone, please just smile.

Lights fade

Act II scene v

Lights up on the fountain, the stage remains empty for a moment, and then Esther enters. She is carrying lunch, as usual. She sits by the fountain. Then she turns, facing in with her feet in the water.

Esther: I came in early today ... because I needed to see you. I wrote down what you said, well, what I could remember anyway ... about your dream ... and flying with angels, and how they are always there but we just don't see them. And then, last night ... I had my dream again. There we were ... David and me, and the kids. We were sitting in our Adirondack chairs watching the clouds in the sky reflected by the water. And it was like it always was ... we were floating between the two skies ... we were flying. Only this time I knew. *She gets up, wades into the fountain and sits down* They told me you went peacefully, and that you even had a smile on your face ... and I laughed and said, "I know." It's almost funny ... I brought a Bible with me this morning ... the Christian one. Because I knew that was where your story would be and I wanted to read it to you. You know the one I told you about when I first knew you ... Acts 9:36-43 ... *She "swims" over to the edge and gets the Bible from her bag* "Now there was at Joppa a certain disciple named Tabitha, which by interpretation is called Dorcas: this woman was full of good works and almsdeeds which she did. And it came to pass in those days, that she was sick and died ... and that is when they called for Peter." You see, Peter was, I guess, conveniently in town, and they brought him to her, where she was laid out and bathed, and then it says that ... they bathed her and laid her in a room up stairs. It's weird how the men who wrote these things were so detailed in some respects and yet so vague ... anyway ... so there they all are, sad and watching, when Peter comes in and then ... "But Peter put them all forth, and kneeled down, and prayed; and turning him to the body said, 'Tabitha'" ... Dorcas ... DJ ... "Arise! And she opened her eyes: and when she saw Peter, she sat up. And he gave her his hand, and lifted her up ..." And I would like to think that they were both smiling.

She sits on the edge for a brief moment then continues ...

Oh, and DJ, you'll like this ... I spoke to Leah, this morning. Right after I visited with you. I told her how weird it was to be in your room, that I never sat in there, that we were always together out here ... by our fountain, our "water feature". I told her I was giving up my work here, that I decided it would be best if I became a burden upon my daughter during this, the planning stages of her wedded life. She was kind, actually, and asked if I was sure I could give this up. I told her to please ... please forgive me and try to understand, but that I just needed today. I needed today to be with you ... and even though you've gone on, I know ... I have faith ... did you hear that DJ? I have faith ... that you are the angel ... pushing and pulling me until I've forgiven myself. So ... I'm going shopping with my daughter tomorrow, for her wedding. And today ... I will sit in this water feature, eat an egg salad sandwich, and perhaps, I'll swim ... and just maybe ... someone will walk by and see me ... and smile.

Lights fade to black

TAKE A LITTLE TIME – Prayer is the Key

Published 2016 by Shechinah Publishing

P.O. Box 22003 Newark, NJ 07101

Copyright © MMXVI by Jenise Williams

Printed in United States of America

Print ISBN: ISBN 978-0-692-71024-1

eBook Editions: Amazon Kindle

Unless otherwise indicated, all scripture quotations and

daily devotion are taken from the *King James Bible* (KJV),

ESV, NIV, NLT Copyright © 2016 public domain

TAKE A LITTLE T

PRAYER IS THE K

The effectual fervent prayer of a righteous
James 5:16

Prayer gives you Strength an

JENISE WILLI